DECLINE OF AMERICA

THE LAST WHITE MAN'S EMPIRE
AND THE RISE OF CHINA: THE BROWN EMPIRE

by Dr. Deshay David Ford, P.H.D.

RoseDog✿Books
PITTSBURGH, PENNSYLVANIA 15238

RoseDog Books
585 Alpha Drive
Suite 103
Pittsburgh, PA 15238
Visit our website at *www.rosedogbookstore.com*

ISBN: 979-8-88527-577-4
eISBN: 979-8-88527-628-3

This book is dedicated to my children and wife, Rachele, Daniel, Edward, my brothers and sisters, and to all of the caring and supportive individuals, who have help me in my journey to reach an understanding of the world and how history impact on future behaviors and decisions.

I would like to give special thank to my foster brother Robert W. Lewis for his support and kindness.

CONTENTS

INTRODUCTION

I was born at Scott, Arkansas on January 14,1948. My parents Maurice and Juanita Ford were hardworking agricultural sharecroppers. My parents were only two generation away from American's enslavement of people of African origin. There were nine siblings in my family with my mother and father making a family of eleven individuals. My brother Harold Maurice Ford was the oldest. I was the second oldest in the family. There was Glenn B. Ford, Philip J. Ford, Robert L. Ford, Wanda Ann Ford (Milburn), Jacqueline Ford (Jackson) and Michael R. Ford. We were a hard working African-American family. My father taught me the respect of hard physical labor. We worked long hours in the agricultural fields in an attempt to earn a living in the racial American South of Arkansas. My mother taught all of the children the importance of getting a good education. My mother had the opportunity of completing high School which was quite an accomplishment for a poor black woman in the segregated apartheid American South.

My father fought in World War two. My father like a lot of Black soldiers were subjected to extreme racism in their military services during the Second World War. My father was subjected to extreme racism in Arkansas on the plantation in which we lived. The future of black people in the segregated American South was very limited. Arkansas like all of the Southern States did not spend much money on the education of black children. Black children were to replace their parents as labors on the white Southern plantations. Black parents and their children did not have any future, but physical labor on the Southern White Plantations.

All of the public schools were racially segregated (Before Brown Vs. Board of Education 1954). My school did not have a library nor a central heating system. The Negro's school's year was coordinated so that negro children could be working in the cotton fields picking cotton in the fall from August to December of the year. My brothers and I had to work in the fields picking cotton and we only attended school when the weather would not allow us to work in the fields picking cotton. During the school of 300 days my brothers and I attended about 80 days. We only attended school during the periods when it was raining and we could not pick cotton.

During the days that I attended school I would not take my recess. I would study my books and practice on the type write to learn how to type. My Uncle Desha Robinson taught me and my brothers how to read by using a large stick. If we missed a word my Uncle Desha would punish us by hitting us with the large stick. My Uncle taught my brothers and I how to read in one week with his large stick. I was in the second grade at seven years old when the U.S. Supreme Court ruled that segregation was un constitutional in the 1954 Brown V. Board of Education case.

I completed high school in 1968. My mother wanted me to attend college. My family could not afford a college education. The large plantation in which my parents sharecropped owner was impressed with my hard work during the periods of time that I would worked in his field chopping grass in cotton fields. Mr. Robert Alexander the Plantation owner invited my mother and I to his home. Mr. Alexander had attended Harvard University. Mr. Alexander told my mother and I about a friend of his name Dr. Graham Roots Hall, Harvard Attorney in Little Rock who needed a worker to help his wife in her garden on the large estate in Little Rock.

I met the Halls and their wonderful Housekeeper Mrs. Winston Elizabeth Minor. Mrs. Minor and I begin a relationships that last for almost twenty years from 1968 to 1996 (Mrs. Minor death). My agreement with Graham and Louise Hall was that I would take care of their large estate during the times they were away and they would pay me a salary and pay for my education at Philander Smith College (Black College) and later at the University of Arkansas, At Little Rock.

Dr. Graham R. Hall was a former Consul-General to India and Australia. Mr. Hall was appointed by President Dwight David Eisenhower to Consul-General to India and Australia l. I met many foreign dignitaries and United States diplomats at Halls. In 1969 I met the British Hugh Foote British Ambassador to United Nations. I met the former United States Ambassador to Russia Sherman Cooper in 1978. In 1980 I met Jeffrey Lewis the United States Ambassador to Nigeria. In 1982 I met Sir Stanley and Lady Burberry from Australian Chief Justice to the Australian Supreme Court. I had the opportunity to meet Paul W. Rockefeller in 1970 the Governor of Arkansas. Governor Rockefeller was the beneficiary of a great deal of affectionate by the Arkansas African-American Community. Mrs. Elizabeth Minor had a friend who was a chef at the Rockefeller Governor mansion in Little Rock. Dr. Graham R. Hall was the attorney for Governor Rockefeller and the Arkansas Republican Party.

During the years I was at the Halls I completed my bachelor degree in Political Science, Master degree in Counseling and psychology, and I begin working on my doctoral degree in Counseling at the University of Arkansas. I also worked as a volunteer in the Governor's campaign of William Jefferson Clinton in 1980 (Clinton won the Presidency in 1991). I had the opportunity to meet Hilary and Bill Clinton. Hilary Clinton worked as a lawyer in the Rose Law Firm in Little Rock. Mrs. Hall's Lawyer G. Gaston Williams was Hilary Clinton's boss at the Rose Law Firm.

Through my many years of employment with Dr. Graham Roots Hall I developed a fondness for foreign policy and world history. Dr. Hall had completed his bachelor at Yale University and his lawyer degree and doctoral of law from Harvard University Law School. My love of learning was encouraged by Graham Hall. On December 30,2012 I completed my doctoral degree in Ministry and Ancient Biblical History at a Seminary in Oxnard, California.

My employment at the Halls as a Property Administrator for twenty years developed my love of American Foreign policy. Dr. Hall and I would discuss his career at the United States State Department working under Dean Acheson the Secretary of State for the Eisenhower's Administration.

Mrs. Winston Elizabeth Minor the Housekeeper to the Graham Halls had the opportunities to travel with the Halls during Mr. Hall's foreign service years in Australia and India. Mrs. Minor was like my mother she reinforced my moral compass and always kept me pointed in the right direction. Louise Boaz Hall Graham Hall's wife was a remarkable woman. Louise and I would engage in great discussions on world affairs. Louise had travelled extensively and she had graduate from Bernard Women college in New York. Louise was a feminist before being a feminist was historically popular. Louise was the boss in the Hall's home. Louise had the ability to make Graham think that he was the boss. Louise made all of the major decisions.

The Halls' had two sons. Lee Boaz Hall was a graduate of Yale University and he travelled all over the world as a foreign journalist. Lee would visit his parents in Little Rock on holidays. Lee would share his travels experiences with me and I would enjoy the stories and his discussing the world leaders that he had personally met. Lee was Skull And Bones at Yale University. Lee was well connected in the Old American ruling class of the Eastern Establishment. Lee was a tall handsome man he was typical of the Old American Anglo-Saxon Patrician ruling class. Lee attended Philip Exeter Prep School in Hanover New Hampshire. Lee Hall graduate from Yale University. Lee was a member of the elite Skull and Bones fraternity the same fraternity as both George Herbert Walker Bush and his son George W. Bush. Both Bushes graduated from Yale University as well as G.H.W. Bush's father Prescott Bush.

In 1970 I received a summer fellowship at Harvard University School of history. I did not accept the fellowship because the fellowship would have interfered with my work duties at the Graham R. Hall in Little Rock, Arkansas.

During my years of employment with the Graham Halls in Little Rock Arkansas I had the Opportunity to meet Hugh Foote the British Ambassador of the United nation in 1969. Mr. Foote was the last British Colonial General during the historical period of dissolution of the British Empire. Ambassador Foote was a house guest of the Graham Hall at their estate in Little Rock, Arkansas. I also had the opportunity to meet the former United States Ambassador to Russia and India John Sherman Cooper form the state of Kentucky while he and his wife were house guest of the Graham Halls in 1978. Mr. Cooper was also a graduate of Harvard Law School as well Graham R. Hall. Mr. Cooper had also been the Senator from the state of Kentucky.

In 1983 I had the opportunity to meet the younger Paul Winthrop Rockefeller before he had become the Lieutenant Governor of the State of Arkansas in 1984.

One of my dearest friend was John M. Roots. Mr. Roots was the first cousin of Graham R. Hall. Mr. Roots was a frequent visitor to the Halls' home in Little Rock, Arkansas. Mr. Roots would share his knowledge and history old China before the Communist came to power in 1949. Mr. Roots' father Logan Roots was a Christian Missionary in China before the Communist came to power in 1949. The new Chinese Communist government leaders dearly loved Bishop Logan Roots because of his love and affection for the common Chinese people (peasants). I met Mr. Roots sister, sister Francis and her husband John Hadden, both were accomplished musicians.

I was the first of my family as a poor black family in the segregated Arkansas to attend college. I started out in college at an all black college called Philander Smith College. I enjoyed my experiences at Philander Smith College. I remember the students, and faculty with love and devotion. I remember Ms. Sarah Gifford. I met Ms. Gifford at Philander Smith College in 1968. Ms. Gifford was an attractive white female who were devoted to the success of her students at an African-American College. My sisters later followed me to college and earned their bachelors and master degrees. I saw Ms. Gifford twenty years later in 1991 at my younger sister graduation from Philander Smith College. Ms. Gifford looked at me and said Deshay you look so old. Ms. Gifford had remembered me as a twenty years old student in 1968. Ms. Gifford also encouraged me to develop my knowledge and expand my knowledge and broaden my world. In 1990 I had the opportunity to go on an European tour of several countries in Europe. My job duties with the Hall was to over see their large estate in Little Rock, Arkansas. The Hall 's home was designed and built by the University of Arkansas Architect Dr. Fay Jones. Dr. Jones studied at the University of Chicago under Frank Lloyd Wright.

While I was a student at Philander Smith College I had the rare opportunity to meet a young Muhammad Ali. Ali was the guest speaker at my college in 1969. Muhammad Ali was a very handsome man the young female students loved him and they hung on every word from his mouth. I had the opportunity to speak to or challenge Muhammad Ali on some of his philosophy. Muhammad won the debate with me concerning his philosophy. My fellow students later told me how much courage that it took for me to challenge a legend. During the twenty years that I worked for the Graham R. Halls I met Mr.

John McCook Roots. Mt. Roots was the first cousin of Graham R. Hall. Mr. Roots father Logan Roots was a missionary in China before the Communist came to power in 1949 under Chair Mao Tseung. Mr. Roots was a Foreign Journalist and he had travelled all over the world. Mr. Roots wrote a book called Chou En Lai the Deputy Premier to Chair Mao Tse-Teung. Mr. Roots could travel back and forth from China before Richard M. Nixon open up China to the Western World.

Graham Hall was a very kind and honorable man. Graham was an old Southern Aristocrat who father Graham Walter Hall had made his fortunate in real estate in the State of Arkansas. Louise Boaz Hall's father Bishop Hiram Boaz was a Bishop in the Methodist Church. Bishop Boaz was the first President and founder of Southern Methodist University in Dallas (Laura Bush the former First lady graduate from Southern Methodist University). Both Graham and Louise came from old Southern aristocracy. George W. Bush's Presidential Library is located on the campus of Southern Methodist University, Dallas, Texas.

Mrs. Elizabeth W. Minor was a physically beautiful woman in 1968. Mrs. Minor was forty-eight years old. Mrs. Minor had worked for the Hall for over forty-five years.Mrs. Minor had accompanied the Halls on the foreign stations while Graham Hall was the Consul-General in the United States Foreign Services. Mrs. Minor told me about her opportunity to meet Althea Gipson the first American woman tennis player to win both the Australian Open, Wimbledon, and the US. Open Tennis Tournaments in 1957.

In 1981 I had the privilege of meeting Dr. Ann Chowning Anthropologist at the University of New Zealand. Dr. Chowning was in Little Rock, Arkansas visiting her brother Robert Chowning. Dr. Chowning and her brother Robert Chowning came from the Arkansas old aristocratic class.

The Hall second and younger son Donald Roots Hall was a professor of Political Science at the University of Arizona at Tucson, Arizona. Donald R. Hall attended Princeton University and the University of Chicago for his doctoral degree. I was blessed by God to be in such an academic environment and received support and encouragement to dev elope my intellect.

I completed my education at the University of Arkansas, At Little rock in 1972. I was a student at the University of Arkansas when the University of Arkansas football team selected their first African-American football player Mr. Jon Richardson in 1970 (Jon Richardson died in Arizona, 2010,at 63 years old).

The reason that I undertook this enormous campaign to write this book I called American the Last White Man's Empire was I saw the similarities of the decline and fall of the ancient Rome Empire. The symptoms of the same problems that existed in the Roman empire exist now exist in The United States Empire.

The Roman's army invaded Britain in A.D. 44 for the purpose of seizing the natural resources and acquiring the British population as slaves. In 2003 A.D. George W. Bush invaded Iraq for the purpose of seizing the Iraq's oil wells. In June 22,1941 A.D Adolph Hitler's army invaded the Soviet Union for the purpose of seizing their oil field and their agricultural lands for the German nation. The Roman were later defeated by the Germanic tribes in 410 A.D. Adolph Hitler's army was defeated at Stalingrad in 1943. The American army was defeated in Iraq by the insurgents after ten years of war (Vietnamese defeated the U.S. Army in 1975, fall of South Vietnam). The Roman, German, and United States ruling classes had become very immoral, decadent, and homosexual.

The Roman Empire like the all empires, Egyptian, Assyrian, Babylonian Greek, Roman, British, and the American Empires become old and decadent and the populations reach a point that they cannot reproduce themselves faster than the oppressed populations (U.S. Latino and Asian population). There are more brown babies born in the US. then there are white babies. The Roman attempted to bring the German populations into the Roman's culture. Their efforts did not work because the Roman people were very racist toward the German tribes. In 378 A.D. a Germanic Tribe called Goths defeated a Roman Army at Adrianople in 378 A.D. The Roman defeat by the Goths begin the decline of the Roman Empire. At the battle of Adrianople in 378 A.D. military technology had changed for the Romans. The battle was historical because it was the first time an army of infantry had been defeated by an army of cavalry. During the first Opium War in 1839 to 1842 the British Army of ten thousand troops defeated a Chinese Nation of a hundred million citizens by being more technologically advanced militarily.

The American Central Intelligence Agency (CIA) has overthrown popular elected governments all over the world. People from the Middle East are now targeting the U.S. for terrorism and bombing. Several countries in South East Asia has overtaken the United States with wealth. The U.S. will reach the point where the Russians were in 1989 after their military campaign in Afghanistan failed. The Russian 's economy could not support a huge military complex and provide for the average Russian citizen.

Dr. Samuel Huntington Professor of history at Harvard University developed a terminology called the Great Diversion. When the Italian explore Marc Polo visited the China in the 14 Century he documented the wealth of the East compared to the poverty in the West. In the 16th Century the West overtook the East and became more wealthy by the utilization of technology and industrialization in the 17 century (Great Britain). In 1839 to 1842 in the First Opium War the British' army of ten thousand soldiers defeated China a nation of one hundred million people by being more technologically advanced. Now modern China is more technologically advanced than Britain and the U.S. The industrialized Countries of Europe believed that China has replaced the U.S. as the new world Super Power.

I have undertaken to examine the reasons why the United States as a world economic and military superpower has been replaced by the Asian giant China in the 21 Century. I do not mean to examine the entire history of the United States, but to examine similar circumstances that led to the decline of other empires and what their decline have in common with the United States.

DECLINE OF AMERICA

THE LAST WHITE MAN'S EMPIRE AND
RISE OF CHINA THE BROWN EMPIRE

PRESIDENT LINCOLN USE OF COMMANDING
CHIEF CLAUSE UNITED STATES CONSTITUTION

The rise of the United States as a world empire begin with the American Civil War. Abraham Lincoln prosecuting the Civil War as the Commanding chief. Lincoln carried out the entire Civil War by using his power under the United States Constitution as the Commanding Chief. President Polk went to Congress and the Senate and he was given a Declaration of War against Mexico in 1846. Prior to Lincoln all of the American President had gone to congress to obtain a Declaration of War against a belligerent state. Congress and the Senate gave President James Madison a Declaration of War against Great Britain in War of 1812. The U.S. Constitution under Article II, Section 2: "The Presidential Powers, Clause 1: refers to the President as the Commander –In-Chief of Army, and Navy of the United States. The President has a free hand in foreign affairs, and he may send men into battle without consulting Congress (Lincoln Civil War, Thurman in Korea, Johnson in Vietnam, Both Bushes in the Middle East, and Obama in Afghanistan). President Lincoln did not go to Congress and secure a Declaration of War to fight the Southern Rebellion. President Lincoln fought the Civil War through his use of his authority under the United States Constitution as the Commanding chief. President Polk the eleventh President went to Congress in 1846 and secure a Declaration of War against Mexico during the Mexican War. President James Madison secure a Declaration of War against Great Britain in the War of 1812.

President Lincoln established a historical precedent by his authority under the Constitution of the Commanding chief Clause in his prosecution of the Civil War against the Confederate States of America From 1861 to 1865. President Franklin Delano Roosevelt obtained a Declaration of War against Japan and Germany after the Japanese attacked Pearl Harbor on December 7,1941.

President Thurman in 1950 also used his powers as the Commanding Chief to fight the Korean War. President Thurman did not seek a Declaration of War from Congress to commit American Troop to repel the North Korean's Army invasion of the South Korea.

President Lyndon Bain Johnson did not obtain a Declaration of War to commit US. Troops to fight in Vietnam in 1965. President obtained the passage of both Houses of the Gulf of Tonkin Resolution which had the effect of committing U.S troops to a police action in Southeast Asia. In 1987 President Ronald Wilson Reagan committed U.S. troops to the invasion of Grenada by using his power as the Commanding Chief under the Constitution.

President George Herbert Walker Bush committed the U.S. troops in 1991 to driving the Iraq's army out of Kuwait. President used his authority under the Constitution as the Commanding Chief. President Bush 's son did not seek a Declaration of War against the Government of Saddam Hussein. In 2003 President George W. Bush the son of George Herbert Walker Bush also utilized his power under the Constitution as Commanding Chief to invade the Government of Saddam Hussein (The invasion of 2003 was an illegal war under the provisions of the United nation).

Abraham Lincoln by his using his power under the Constitution as Commanding Chief he historically established the foundation of the American Empire. After the assassination of Julius Caesar in 44 B.C. Augustus his nephew came to power and begin the Roman Empire. Augustus ended the Republic by becoming Emperor and the Roman Senate surrendered their power passing laws, thereby, the Senate gave Augustus absolute power over the army and the Roman State in 31 B.C.

After Abraham Lincoln American Presidents did not have to go to congress to seek a Declaration of War against another state. The future Presidents could used their power under the U.S. Constitution as the Commanding Chief and their roles as Imperialist presidents.

President Lincoln being the first President to fight a war without a Declaration War. President Lincoln using his power as Commanding Chief set American on a course of Empire building. Democratic States are by nature cannot be empires. Empires are by nature ran by one imperial king or emperor who make all of the governmental decisions. The British Empire of the 18th century was ran by the king through his Prime Ministers (Queen Victoria). The King did not have to go a Parliament to request the power to prosecute the war against the American colonists. The King George III had to request funds to run his military operation in the American Revolution against the colonists.

The Roman Republic prior to the assassination of Julius Caesar in 44 B.C. was a Republican Government. The country was ruled by the Senate. The Republic would in military emergency select a citizen and grant him dictator power temporarily to handle the emergency circumstance (Cincinnatus, 519-430 B.C.). After the military emergency had been alleviated the citizen's dictator powers would be relinquished. After the assassination of Julius Caesar and the defeat of Mark Anthony and Cleopatra in Naval Battle of Actium in 31 B.C. by Octavian and Marcus Agrippa the Roman Republic cease to exist.

The German people republic after the First World was the Weimar Republic. In 1933 Adolph Hitler came to power as the head of government and he had the Bundestag enact the Enabling Act which gave Hitler absolute power over the nation.

In 1965 United States Congress gave President Johnson the authority to use American troops in Vietnam through the Gulf of Tonkin Resolution. The Gulf of Tonkin Resolution was not a Declaration of War. The Gulf of Tonkin Resolution was the authority for a temporary police or military campaign by the President. President Lincoln by using his powers under the Constitution as Commanding Chief set the United States on the path to Empire.

THE ROMAN EMPIRE

The Roman Republic begin in 509 B.C. The Roman's citizen did away with the monarchy and selected a citizen representative type of government. When there was time of national emergency the Roman citizens would select a man to lead the country until the time that the emergency had past. The person would be appointed as dictator for a short period of time until the national emergency circumstance had passed. The appointment of a Dictator would end after emergency circumstance had passed. In 55 B.C Julius Caesar was appointed Dictator to deal with a crisis. The Senate fearing that Julius Caesar wanted to become Dictator for life the senators with Brutus conspired to kill Julius Caesar. On 44 B.C. Senators with Brutus assassinated Julius Caesar. The Roman's civil war begin with Octavian defeating Anthony and Cleopatra 3 1 B.C and becoming the Roman first Emperor. When Abraham Lincoln asserted the power of Commanding Chief Lincoln had become the first American Julius Caesar and the beginning of the American Empire.

GREAT DIVERGENCE

The Great Divergence, a term coined by Samuel Huntington (also known as the European miracle, a term by Eric Jones in 1981), refers to the process by which the Western World (i.e. Western Europe and the parts of the New World where its people became the dominant populations) over came pre-modern weaker countries and emerged irrefutably during the 19th century as the most powerful and wealthy world civilization of the time, eclipsing Qing China, Mughal India, Tokugawa Japan and The Ottoman Empire.

The Great Divergence as Professor Huntington has named it was when the Western Europe over came the Asiatic Civilizations and Middle Eastern civilizations to become the dominant civilization for 500 hundred years (1600-2013). The Chinese invented gun powder and the cannon. The English was the first country to place the cannon on a ship. This process was accompanied and reinforced by the Age of Discovery and the subsequent rise of the colonial empires (Great Britain), the Age of Enlightenment, the commercial, the Scientific Revolution and finally the Industrial Revolution.

Before the Great Divergence, the core developed areas included East Asia, Western Europe, the Indian subcontinent, and the Middle East. In each of these core areas, differing political and cultural institutions allowed varying degrees of development. China, Western Europe, and Japan had developed to a relatively high level and began to face constraints on energy and land use, while India still possessed large amounts of unused resources. Shifts in government policy from Mercantilism to laissez-faire liberalism aided Western development (Slave States.Great Britain, Holland, and the Spanish Empire). The European civilizations were the first major countries utilized people as slaves because of the color of their skins. The Chinese civilizations, Indian, Middle Eastern civilizations never used color of people skin color as a racial justification for utilizing people's labor. The Great Wall of Chinese was not built with slave labor utilizing skin color as the justification for slavery. The White House where President Obama resides as the United States president was built with the labor of slaves. The Spanish utilized slave labor in the New World. The English when they conquered India the English used the native people as slave labor in building India into a commercial venture for the British Empire. The British introduced opium in Chinese as a result of the Opium War of 1839-1842. The Opium addiction in China was created by the British Commercial class to make money for the British Empire. The British defeated the Chinese and opened the Chinese's ports up for British trade in opium. The British commercial interest caused the Chinese addiction to opium and the famous opium dens in China. The British through the Opium Treaty obtained a hundred lease on the territory of Hong Kong. Hong Kong became a British's colony like America in the New World.

The Roman Empire like the British Empire was build on conquest of small and large countries. Rome started out like Great Britain as a small tribe of people forming a country by conquering their neighbors and securing their land and natural resources(Romans conquered England in 55B.C Julius Caesar expedition). Britain was conquered by the Roman Emperor Claudius in 44 A.D.

The American Empire begin with a concept called Manifest Destiny. The Americans Imperialists led by President James Polk wanted to extend United States from the Pacific Ocean to the Atlantic Ocean. James Polk campaigns for the U.S Presidency was supporting expansion of U.S. into Mexico. James Polk, on his inauguration night confided to his Secretary of the Navy that his principal objective of his presidency was the acquisition of California, which Mexico had refused to sell to the United States at any price. James Polk a Southern wanted the new territory for the expansion of slavery into the new territory.

As early as 1845 James Polk promises Texas he would support moving the historical Texas and Mexico Border at the Nueces River 150 miles south to the Rio Grande provided Texas agreed to join the Union. Texas War with Mexico 1836 was about white settlers bring slaves into Texas. The Mexican Constitution of 1824 abolished slavery. The American whites colonies were bring their slaves into Texas which was Mexican's territory. The American colonists were looking for new agricultural land to grow cotton. The traditional border between Texas and Mexico was recognized as the border. James Polk ordered American's troops to march into Mexican inhabited territory causing Mexicans to flee their villages for their lives and abandon their crops in terror. James Polk ordering the American troops to the Rio Grande, into territory inhabited by Mexicans, was clearly a provocation (Howard Zinn, Theft of Mexican Territory). President Polk had incited war by sending American soldiers into was disputed territory, historically controlled and inhabited by Mexicans. In 1846 An American Colonel Hitchcock, commander of the 3rd infantry regiment, writes in his diary the United States are the aggressors we have not one particle of the right to be here, It looks as if the government sent a small force on the purpose to bring on a war, so as to have pretext for taking California and as much of this country (Mexico) as it chooses, my heart is not in this business.

The British in the Balfour Declaration promised the Jews that if they help the British win the First World War against Germany and her allies Britain would grant the Jews of Europe Palestine (James A. Balfour, 1917, British Foreign Office). There was no Mexican's troops present. Violence erupts between Mexican and American troops south of the Nueces River. President James Polk claimed that Mexican's troops fired the first shot.

Abraham Lincoln repeatedly challenges President Polk to name the exact spot where Mexican first attacked American Troops. President Polk never met Lincoln's challenge. President urges Congress to declare war. Congressman Abraham Lincoln opposed the declaration of war against Mexico for the purpose of seizing Mexican's territory by American aggression (George W. Bush, Gulf War 2003-2013). Congresswoman Barbara Lee of Berkeley, California opposed granting George W. Bush permission to invade Iraq for the purpose of securing the oil fields.

Congressman Abraham Lincoln speaking in a session of Congress, stated that the President unnecessarily and unconstitutionally commenced a war with

Mexico by marching an army into the midst of a peaceful Mexican settlement, frightening the inhabitants away, leaving their growing crops and other property to destruction, to you may appear perfectly amiable, peaceful, unprovoked procedure; but it does not appear to us. After the war was under way, the American Press comments: February 11,1847. The Congressional Globe " reports: We must march to ocean, we must march from Texas straight to the Pacific Ocean, it is the destiny of the white race, it is the destiny of the Anglo-Saxon Race. Before the United States got involved in the Indo-China War an American Colonel was talking to the French General after the French had lost the war in ten years of fighting the Indo-China Vietnam Nationalists," that the United States would win the war in nine months, because Americans were a superior white race and the Vietnamese were an Inferior race of people (David Halberstam, Best and Brightest, 1972).

In March of 1954 The Vietnamese General Giap begin surround the French troop at Dien Bien Phu and the battle went on for several months. The French realized that they could not win the battle under French General Navarre. Finally on May 7, 1954 the French surrendered after fifty-five days of resistance. The United States entered the Vietnam war in 1965 with passing of the Gulf of Tonkin Resolution giving President Johnson the approval to use United States Troops. July of 1975 the US was defeated in the Vietnam war. The North Vietnam's Army seize the United States Embassy in South Vietnam. The defeat of the United States in Vietnam brought to a historical end of the white European Empires dominance in Asia.

From 1846-1848 the United States Army battles Mexico, not just enforcing the new Texas Border at the Rio Grande but capturing Arizona, New Mexico, Utah, Colorado, and California as well as marching as far south as Mexico city. Mexico surrendered on U.S terms and the US took ownership of New Mexico, California an expanded Texas, and more for a token payment of $15 million, which leads the Whig intelligencer to report: "We take nothing by conquest, thank God," United States invasion of Iraq the U.S. claimed that the U.S. were liberators not conquerors,(G. W. Bush's War 2003-2013).

FIVE LIES TOLD BY BUSH TO START A WAR (2003, 43 THIRD PRESIDENT)

All of these and many other lies by Bush, and the language of the law, are factually documented in great detail within the book, Proof of Guilt. It is a fact of U.S. law that if it can be proven that a President purposely told lies to cause a war that killed people, those lies demonstrate criminal intent and killing automatically constitutes the crime of murder by President Bush (James Polk lies about the starting of war with Mexico 1846). The five lies:

1. How Bush planned his Iraq war four years in advance, in 1999, and knew then that Iraq had no (Weapon of Mass Destruction) WMD, or any intent to attack; that was just a lie, a pre-planned false pretext for an attack.

2. Bush's own 2003 admission that what he had said, pre-war, about the deadly threat from Iraq was a deliberate fraud; 18 months of saying it without any evidence was no accident.

3. The deliberately falsified intelligence report Bush sent to Tony Blair pre-war that, had it not been falsified, British intelligence said "we would never have gone to war.

4. The unconscionable falsification, by his own admission, that Bush swore to Congress was true the day before his Iraq attack ;that illegally allowed him to attack the very next day.

5. The widely ignored United Nations agency announcement two weeks before Bush's attack and after months of investigation that absolutely none of Bush's falsely claimed Iraq weapons actually existed.

An independent review of the U.S. government 's anti-terrorism response after September 11 attacks reported Tuesday (4/16/2013) that it is indisputable the United States engaged in torture and that George W. Bush administration bears responsibility (New York, Times, 2017)

PRELUDE TO A CATASTROPHE:

On March 20, 2003, G.W. Bush began the worst crime in American history. Over the next 4 years he would lead us, the people of America, to murder, wound and displace over 4.4 million people with absolutely justification except as a terrorist act. By definition, that made us, American people, the worst terrorist organization in the entire history in the world for the years 2003-2007. We were both the terrorists and the victims. This is a story about truth and lies, justice and injustice. It is the chronicle of the twisted ideology of a privilege few who, for many years used massive fraud to con the public and hundreds of thousands of war victims into fighting a blood and guts war over an illusionary purpose, guided by deliberately fraudulent public pretext.

This same fraud was intentionally employed by Bush et al to propagandize that questionable purpose, and hide the actual truth of Bush's criminality. Bush et al did by this by adopting his own set of "phony facts". The main one came from the neoconservatives phony 1996 Iraq Plan that Bush had adopted in 1999. Bush told us its fraudulent myth that Iraq threatened to attack us with WMD (Weapon of Mass Destruction), and that we urgently needed to attack them first to save ourselves from their claimed nuclear attack. That intentional outright fraud was then presented to the American public in a massive and persuasive propaganda campaign. The whole country then made national decisions, logically based upon these "phony facts" of the fraud campaign. Those predictably misguided decisions led to premeditated criminal war on Iraq : a bloody disaster!

Unfortunately the public is relatively unaware of how truly dangerous "political phony facts," because they were kept hidden from sight and sound. And by the absence of appropriate legal action.

Congress Barbara Lee of Berkeley, California voted against giving President Bush the approval to go to war in Iraq in 2003. Abraham Lincoln voted against declaring war on Mexico on 1846 as requested by then President James K. Polk.

On August 7,1964 United States Congress passed the Gulf of Tonkin Resolution giving President Johnson the approval to use American Troops in Vietnam. President Lyndon B. Johnson had ordered Central Intelligent Agency to support South Vietnamese 's forces operations against North Vietnamese territory had provoked the North Vietnamese forces to initiate an attack on what they thought was the South Vietnamese and American CIA forces. President Johnson informed Congress that American Warship the Maddox had been attacked in International waters. The President asked for the a Resolution to use American forces to prevent further aggression by the North Vietnamese.

The House passed the Gulf of Tonkin Resolution 414 to 0 and the Senate passed the Resolution 88 to 2. Senators Wayne Morse of Oregon and Senator Ernest Gruening of Alaska opposed the Resolution. Barbara Lee of Berkeley, California opposed giving President George W. Bush the approval to go to war in Iraq in 2003. Congresswoman Lee received death threats for opposing George W. Bush rush to war in Iraq.

On March 19,2013 was the anniversary of George W. Bush going to war in Iraq. The United States lost nearly 5,000 soldiers killed and over 40,000 young men and women with permanent injuries. There was over 200,000 Iraq's citizens who were killed. Bush and his co-conspirators were hoping to pay for the war by seizing the Iraq's oil fields. The Iraq War was the United States Stalingrad. January of 1943 the entire German's 6th Army under Field Marshall Von Paulius surrendered to the Russian Army. The destruction of the 6th Army was the greatest military disaster for the Adolph Hitler's Army. Hitler's Army never recovered from the disaster at Stalingrad. The American's Army also will not recover from their Iraq Stalingrad of 2003-2013. Adolph Hitler purpose for invading Russia was to seize their oil. George W. Bush's purpose for invading Iraq was to seize their oil.

The British Empire faced the critical circumstance at the beginning of the twentieth Century. The enlargement of the empire and the wars which accompanied it attracted enormous public interest in Britain. The process coincided with a widespread revision of ideas about empire and its future. Rethinking the empire had been stimulated by two speculative books, Sir Charles Dilke's Great Britain (1869) and the selling The Expansion of England (1882) by Sir John Seeley. Both offered consolation for those who were apprehensive about Britain's future. For Seeley the empire was the main source of British strength and its expansion and unity were vital for the nation's survival as a great power. In the modern world size equaled strength and vitality, both America and Germany had grown in area and population during (China great population 2.1 billion people) the past twenty years and had accordingly increased in strength. The sinews of British power were its colonies, particularly the white dominions, (White man burden to govern the colored races of world)which were extension of Britain. If, as Seeley hoped, they continued to expand then Britain could hold her own in the world and eventually outdistance her new rivals.

10

The British Empire was an expression of what Seeley considered to be the special genius of the Anglo-Saxon race, that is the British (America new White Empire). Social Darwinism was now fashionable and its theories, a rough and ready transfer of Darwinism principles from the world of plants and animals to that of men, suggested that certain races were better fitted to survive and flourish than others (United States used same philosophy to enslave African-Americans until the Civil War, 1861-1865). Leaving on one side the pertinent question as to who exactly was the Anglo-Saxons, and late nineteenth-century imperialists usually did (President James Polk used same doctrine to seize Mexico's territory, 1846-1848), there was a common agreement that their assumed progeny, the British, represented a super-race. This conclusion could be justified in terms of material, scientific and intellectual progress and adaptability. The fact that the Anglo-Saxons had dispersed across the globe and mastered their environment added to the general feeling that they were ideally qualified to rule.

Notions of racial superiority blended with arguments for imperial unity to produce an Ideology for the new imperialism. It suited the times, since it offered Britain a chance to reverse the decline of its international power and revive a torpid economy. After all, in 1884 three million Australians consumed 23 million pounds worth of British goods (After World War II U.S. had large trade surplus with world). In the twenty-first century China has the largest balance of trade with world. The Chinese economy has exceeded the U.S regarding international trade. Here was with U.S. not only a valuable market, but a country whose ties of kinship, language and institutions were with Britain. Striking proof of this provided the following year when New South Wales sent troops to serve alongside British and Indian units in the Sudan.

The most significant convert to the imperial creed of Dilke and Seeley was Joseph Chamberlain. He was probably the most able politician of his time and certainly the most restless and difficult to label. In appearance he looked like archetypal aristocrat with elegant features, a monocle and a fresh orchid in his buttonhole. Chamberlain was in fact a Birmingham businessman who progressed from Radical Lord Mayor with fierce republican views to a liberal minister under Gladstone, and in 1895, Colonial Secretary in a Conservative government. During the course of his political perambulations he split two parties, the Liberals in 1886 and the Conservatives in 1904, a unique achievement which says much for his influence.

Of all the causes which Chamberlain embraced, that of the empire was the most deeply felt and longest lasting. The United States had the similar character in Theodore Roosevelt who was also committed to the new American Empire. Roosevelt encouraged and support the Spanish War of 1898. Roosevelt promoted American uniqueness and the superiority of the American white race. Chamberlain attachment to the idea of imperial unity, as well as frustration with Gladstone's indifference towards social reform, drove Chamberlain to desert the Liberals over the Irish Home Rule in 1886. Therefore, Chamberlain led his splinter Unionist towards a coalition with the Conservatives, reserving for himself what had hitherto been a minor cabinet office, Colonial Secretary. Chamberlain brand of imperialism was amalgam of older notions of disseminating civilization and modern concepts of race.

In 1893, when Britain had accepted a protectorate over Uganda, Chamberlain told the Commons that the country welcomed the new addition to the empire (President James Polk, seizing Mexico's territory after the Mexican War of 1846-1848). THE English people were, Chamberlain stated were well matched to the tasks of spreading The British White Civilization since they were animated by all traditions of the past, and by what Chamberlain called that spirit of adventure and enterprise distinguishing the Anglo-Saxon race (which) has made us peculiarly fit to carry out the working of colonization. The United States utilized the same philosophy in their wars against the Western Indian Tribes from 1862 to 1892 (Wounded Knee Massacre1892, Dakota Territory).

It was essential that the Anglo-Saxon race should understand the qualities that it needed to foster if it was to fulfill its historic destiny (Manifest Destiny 1846-1848 War with Mexico). Most importantly, the young had (American white race) had to be given models of how the Anglo-Saxon should behave and which of his innate virtues he should cultivate and how.A generation of university teachers, schoolmasters, clergymen (Billy Graham supported United States military campaign in Vietnam War 1965-1975) poets, journalists and fiction writers concentrated their minds and energies on popularizing the cult of the new imperialism (Hollywood, New York Times, and Television media supported George W. Bush invasion of Iraq in 2003).

At its heart lay the concept of Anglo-Saxon manhood (Lyndon B. Johnson statement that the Vietnamese testing American manhood), an abstraction compounded in equal parts of patriotism, physical toughness, skill at team games (American Football, Central Intelligence Agency recruiting from Yale, George Herbert Walter Bush, William F. Buckley, class of 1948), a sense of fair play (sometime called sportsmanship), self-discipline, selflessness, bravery and daring.

The ground had been well prepared for the apostles of the Anglo-Saxon ideal. Since 1840s the public schools had undergone a revolution, started by Dr. Thomas Arnold of Rugby, which transformed the habits of mind of the, idle and upper classes. Arnold and his acolytes sought to instill Christian Christian altruism into their pupils and direct their ambition and aggression towards the playing field. The public schoolboy, educated according to the Arnoldian Code, also learned how to control himself and control others through the prefectorial system, a perfect preparation for the ruling and chastising the empire's lesser breeds. Intelligence mattered less than the acquisition of character activity was largely restricted to otiose and repetitive exercises in the languages of two former imperial powers, Greece and Rome. The Romans under Emperor Claudius conquered Britain in A.D. 45. Britain was an imperial out post of the Roman Empire for 400 hundred years (476 Last Roman Emperor Romulus August). The Roman empire like the United States had out posts all over the Mediterranean World and outside of the Mediterranean World (Britain, London Roman outpost until 4 Century A.D.).The end product was a Christian gentleman with a stunted imagination, who played by the rules and whose highest aims was to serve others. If he had to earn his living, he elected to become an army or navy officer (Sir Winston Churchill), a senior civil servant (Author James Balfour, British Foreign Services, Balfour Manifesto 1917 granted the Jews right to Palestine), clergyman, a barrister, or joined a branch of the Indian or Colonial Administration (Hugh Foot, Last British Colonial General, Little rock, Arkansas 1969).

By 1880 a generation had passed into manhood with an outlook which made them ideally suited to govern the empire and fight its wars (Yale University produced George H.W. bush, class of 48, William F. Buckley, Willie Roosevelt, Wild Bill Donovan the founder of the modern Central Intelligence

Agency, 1946). The highest examples of this feeling of God Right for Anglo-Saxon race to rule were represented in a stained-glass window in the chapel of Sedbergh school which showed three Christian heroes of the empire: Sir Henry Lawrence, a warrior proconsul in India, and two martyrs, General Gordon and Bishop Patterson, a South Sea missionary. The ideals of Arnoldian Christian manliness merged easily with those of the new imperialism.

President James Polk during the War with Mexico 1846-1848 seizure of Mexican's territory and the philosophy of Manifest Destiny and Theodore Roosevelt promoting war with Spain to seizure Spanish territory was the begin of the American Empire.

World War I and II were the end of the British Empire. George W. Bush's Iraq War was the end of the American Empire (Iraq War, 2003-2013). The United States defeat in Iraq was historically similar to the defeat of the Germany Army in 1943 at Stalingrad. After the German's defeat and surrender at Stalingrad(Germany General (Friedrich Von Paulus) the army was fighting just to survive.

 The United States Military does not have the will nor resources to fight and defeat the North Korean 's Army. The Roman 's Army defeat at the hands of the Goths at Adrianople in 378 A.D ended the Roman Army perceived invincibility.

The defeat of Hitler's army at the gate of Stalingrad and the United States Army in Iraq end these armies perceived invincibility. The Roman military like the British, German., and the American military which had philosophies of racial superiority over their opponents which led to their own destruction. The American army defeat in Vietnam end the perception of American Army invincibility.

The German army defeat at Stalingrad end the German's army perception of invincibility. After Stalingrad the German's army was on the defensive and it ended in their capitol of Berlin in 1945.

The defeat of George W. Bush's war (2003-2012) also ended the perception of the invincibility of the American's army. The North Korea's leader is threatening the United States with war on the Korean Peninsula. The United States cannot hope to defeat the North Korean's military. The North Koreans have the nuclear weapons, therefore the U.S. is not a threat to the North Koreans.

President Obama is attempting to negotiate an agreement between the State of Israel and the Palestinians territory. The British and French during the First World War in the Sykes-Picot Agreement officially known as the Asia Minor Agreement, was a secret agreement between the governments of the United Kingdom and France, with the assent of Russia, defining their proposed spheres of influence and control in the Middle East should the Triple Entente succeed in defeating the Ottoman Empire during World War 1. The negotiation of the treaty occurred between November 1915 and March 1916. The agreement effectively divided the Arab provinces of the Ottoman Empire outside the Arabian Peninsula into areas of the future British and French control or influence. The terms were negotiated by the French diplomat Francois Georges-Picot and the British Sir Mark Sykes. The Russian Tsarist government was a minor party to the Sykes-Picot agreement, and when, following the Russian Revolution of October 1917, the Bolsheviks exposed the agreement, the British were embarrassed, the Arabs dismayed and the Turks delighted. Britain was allocated control of areas roughly comprising the coastal strip between the sea and River Jordan, Jordan, Southern Iraq, and a small area including the ports of Haifa to Acre, to allow access to the Mediterranean. France was allocated control of South-eastern Turkey, Northern Iraq, Syria and Lebanon. Russia was to get Istanbul, the Turkish Straits and the Ottoman Armenian Vilayets.

The British entered China after the Napoleonic War era. For over three thousand years, until the late-thirteenth-century arrival of Marco Polo, the Chinese Empire had lived out its life virtually unknown to the outside world and unaffected by it. Even when the great Venetian explorer returned to Europe with his tales of wonder, he was generally disbelieved, and was in fact haled before the Inquisition for bearing false witness.

Then, beginning in the sixteenth century, the Portuguese, followed at intervals by the Dutch, Spanish, English and the French, established trading posts along the coasts of South China, Japan and the Philippines. But three hundred years they were successfully contained and kept at arm's length by the Imperial Court at Peking. Not until the Napoleonic Era, from which England emerged as the mightiest power on earth, did any foreign nation feel herself strong enough to force the issue. After Waterloo in 1815, England felt able to act, and throughout the next Quarter century sought a plausible pretext.

By then long in control of India, the British found civilization of the poppy there to be commercially profitable, and for many years carried on a contraband export trade in opium along the South china Coast. U.S traders selling Persian opium were second in this commerce. The Peking government, understandably concerned by its people's growing demand for the drug and its consequent menace to Chinese society, moved early in 1839 to impound and destroy thousand chests of opium at canton. Seeing in this the desire pretext, British warships went into action, silence the forts defending the icy, sank the primitive armed junks sent against them, and eventually, forced China to submit (The Chinese called this period in their history the period of the Great humiliation). The United States was built with the slave labor of Black people from Africa. The White House where President Obama and his family reside in were build by slave labor (1619-20th –Century).

The English victory in what has become known to history as the Opium War (1840-1842), began what every Chinese to this day refers to as China's Century of Humiliation at the hands of the west. Hong Kong in the South was seized, and Weihaiwei in the North, and the proud but helpless Peking government was forced to open selected "Treaty Ports to Western trade. Thus China's isolation, eventually doomed under any circumstances, was in fact ended by an incident so morally indefensible that it has become a byword for infamy to every Chinese schoolchild and a treasure trove for Communist propagandists around the globe.

Other European powers eventually followed Britain into Asia. France took Indo-China (Vietnam, Cambodia); Germany annexed Tsingtao, port of Shantung, the province where Confucius was born; Japan, Korea and Taiwan. Russia seized Vladivostok, the Soviet Far East and Soviet Central Asia, penetrated deeper into Manchuria, and turned hungry eyes on Mongolia.

The devastating Tai-ping (Great Peace) Rebellion in mid-century, China's first popular protest against these foreign depredations, was eventually suppressed with the help of Britain's General Chinese Gordon. It leader, Hung Hsiu-chuan, characterized himself as the younger brother of Jesus and formulated a revolutionary ideology that was Chinese version of Protestant

Christianity (General Charles Gordon, a regular British Army Officer and a devout Christian, played a prominent leadership role in the final suppression of the Pseudo-Christian-oriented Tai-ping rebellion 1851-1864). Gordon later died defending Britain's imperial interests at Khartoum, in Africa's Sudan. Gordon has been regarded as a hero by the British, if not by either the Chinese or Sudanese (White American Southerners viewed Dr. Marin Luther King as an enemy of white racial supremacy). Hung Hsiu-ch'uan came close to success, and failed only after fourteen years (1851-1864) of civil war at the cost of forty millions lives. Historically, the Tai-ping Rebellion (now renamed the Tai-ping Revolution" by Peking), was in many ways a forerunner of the better-known Boxer Rebellion at the turn of the century (1901). Hung was much admired by Chou and later China's later Communist leaders because of his radical social reforms such as the redistribution of land, the abolition of slavery and the sale of women and children, the outlawing of foot binding, prostitution, arranged marriages, polygamy, and the importation of opium. These reforms, and participation by the army in agriculture and industry, foreshadowed many of the reforms reinstituted a century later under the People's Republic.

In 1900 during the boxer Rebellion and international army (United States Army) relieved the besieged Legation Quarter of Peking, turning it into a final foreign concession. As the twentieth century begin, China was hardly more than a geographical expression. Foreign warships patrolled her rivers, harbors and coastal waters. White men were not answerable in any Chinese court. Signs in a Shanghai park read: "Chinese and dogs not admitted " (U.S. cities blacks not permitted at sundown).

The hated foreigner was of course only half the story. China's bitter colonialist yoke was more than matched by the oppressions of her own feudalistic government and society.

"Every year, in China of my youth, John McCook Roots book, Chou, An informal Biography of China Chou En –Lai five to ten million people would die from preventable causes-flood, famine, disease, Civil war". The infant mortality rate ran at a staggering two hundred per thousand live births. The nationwide TB rate was estimated at 6 per cent (1949-1976 the Communists have eliminated a majority of all of these health problems)." John McCook Roots stated that during his school days, the police of the international Settlement, on winter nights, would often collect in garbage vans a couple of hundred nameless corpses off the streets. In the cities beggars were everywhere and the filth and stench indescribable. No national illiteracy figures could verified, but all agreed they were astronomical, running well over 95 percent.

Some knowledge of the scenes and atmosphere of the treaty-port China is essential if Westerns are to understand how completely all Chinese in the People's Republic have repudiated their Colonialist past when White Men dominated their country. Chou En-Lai knew colonialist Shan well during his underground years there. Neal Hunter (Chou An Informal Biography of China's Legendary Chou En Lai, John Mc Cook Roots) an Australian who taught Foreign Language in Shanghai from 1965-1967, paints a vive picture of the race course, which I well remember from my school days.

The physical center of colonial Shanghai was the British race course. This spacious oval of green grass acted as lung in the middle of the grimy metropolis. The Communists, with a touch of irony, had converted one of the grandstands into a public library. I would sit and read in the former club-rooms where Englishman had presumably discussed the White Man 's Burden over gin and tonic. Outside the windows the tiers of seats were still there, and I would picture great crowd assembled for of sport of kings, or perhaps a more select audience for the cricket that was played on the oval circumscribed by the track.

That how Shanghai was: the master race, center stage, playing a game which it alone understood; and the natives unable to advance beyond the magic circle of the race track, where they were offered the tantalizing but remote specter of wealth.

Life for the Chinese in old Shanghai cannot have been much fun. The Communists swept into power by an army of paupers certainly failed to appreciate the sporting mentality of Western business. With the zeal of angels, they set about suppressing opium, prostitution, child labor, gangsters.

China under the control of the Western powers were an oppressive environment of the ordinary Chinese persons. The Chinese were slaves in their own country to the white European powers including the United States. The United States financially benefited from the Opium War from 1839 to 1842. American businesses men made substantial amount of money on the creation of the opium dens in China. The British Empire was financed by the opium trade and the misery and suffering of poor Chinese citizens using the British's opium.

When the Boxer Rebellion in 1900 the United States sent a troop of United States Marine to aid the white European powers in their campaigns to suppress the native Chinese 's efforts to expel the white European powers from their country.

The United States had first allowed Chinese labors to come into the United States on a temporary bases to (1840s) fill a need supply of labors to work on the international rail road building project. The U.S. Government never intended for the Chinese labors to remain in the U.S. The U.S. officials felt that the Chinese Race were so different that they could never be successfully introduced into the American White Racial blood pool. So in 1882 the United States Congress passed a Law. The Act was called the Chinese Exclusion Act of 1882. The United States Government only allowed Chinese men to come to the U.S. The Chinese could not bring over their wives or females companions. A lot of the Chinese men mated with local women of color (Black, Mexican, and native women).

The Asian people have a valid concerned about the United States using the nuclear bomb. The United States is the only country that has used the nuclear bomb against an adversary. The United States used the nuclear bombs against the Japanese empire in August of 1945. During the Korean War General Douglas Macarthur asked then President Harry Thurman to use the nuclear bomb against Communist China. The United States has a history of racial discrimination against Asian people.

In 1871 there was a massacre of Chinese people in Los Angeles in 1871. The Chinese massacre of 1871 was racially motivated on October 24,1871, a mob of over 500 Caucasians entered Los Angeles 's Chinatown to attack and eventually murder Chinese American residents of the city. The riots took place on Calle de los Negros (known colloquially as nigger Alley), which later became Los Angeles Street. Every Chinese-occupied building on the block was ransacked and almost every resident was attacked or robbed. Estimates of the number of dead vary, but between 20 and 23 Chinese residents were killed. At the time, there were only 200 Chinese living in Los Angeles.

The dead Chinese in Los Angeles were hanging at three places near the heart of the downtown business section of the city; from wooden awning over the sidewalk in front of a carriage shop; and from the cross-bean of a wide gate leading into a lumber yard a few blocks away from the other two locations. One of victims hung without his trousers and minus a finger on his left hand.

The event was triggered by the accidental killing of Robert Thompson, a Caucasian man, who was caught in the cross-firing between two men arguing over the affections of a young woman.

However, the underlying causes are generally considered to be economic. The riots were part of a growing movement of Anti-Chinese discrimination in California (There similar anti-Chinese racial riots in San Francisco the same year of 1871). In 1882 The United States Senate and Congress Passed what is the Chinese Exclusion Act. The American leaders felt the Chinese race could not be integrated into the American culture with the white race. The root economic causes were the unstable economy after the American Civil War which led to high unemployment in California and other Western states. The man who actually shot Thomas escaped and very few of the rioters were punished. The event was well-reported on the East Coast as newspapers there labeled Los Angeles a "blood stained Eden".

The North Koreans have a historical reason to be afraid of the United States. During the Korean War General Douglas McArthur requested from President Thurman the approval to used the Atom Bomb against the Chinese military in 1952. President Thurman were afraid that if the United States used the Atom Bomb the Soviet Union also use the Atom Bomb. The existence of the nuclear bomb by the Russians prevented the United States from using the nuclear bomb on another Asian race.

General William Westmoreland requested the approval to use the nuclear bomb from President Lyndon Bain Johnson in 1967. President Johnson was afraid that if the U.S. used the nuclear bomb the Chinese would also used their nuclear bomb (The Tragedy of Vietnam, Causes and Consequences, Patrick J. Hearden, 2006).

The current military crisis between the United States and North Korean will not lead to war. Both sides possess nuclear weapons which would destroy both the U.S. and North Korean's Civilizations. Imperialist Empire will only go to war with small countries that they believe that they can destroy without suffering any damages to their societies. The United States in 2003 attacked

Iraq because they were a small powerless country which did not present a threat to the American Homeland. The North Koreans present and immediate threat to the United States Home Land. After the American Military defeats in Iraq and Afghanistan the United States Army is in no condition to fight a land war in Asia with a North Korean's Army of three millions soldiers. The U.S. as a declining Empire will negotiate our way out of a military confrontation with the North Koreans and maintain their pride and symbols of a great imperialist power (Dr. D. Ford, end of US, imperialist power, 2013).

SEPTEMBER 11, 1973 CIA COUP IN CHILE

September 11, 1973 is now engraved on the consciousness of Americans. Yet for the South American country of Chile, the date has a different and much more tragic significance. It was on that day in 1973 that the democratically-elected government of Salvador Allende was overthrown in a CIA backed military coup. Augusto Pinochet seized power. General Pinochet was backed and supported by the CIA.(1953 President Eisenhower approved the overthrow of the Iran Democratic government of Mohammad Mossadegh by CIA and British Petroleum, BP). The United States through the Central Intelligence Agency had overthrown the Democratic elected government of Mohammad Mossadegh in 1953. The primary reason for overthrowing Mossadegh was he stated that he would nationalize Anglo-Iranian Oil company (BP). The coup was led by an agent name Kermit Roosevelt the grandson of President Theodore Roosevelt. The CIA leaned on a young, insecure Shah to issue a decree dismissing Mossadegh as the elected Prime Minister. There were some 300 people died in fire fights in the streets of Tehran. Mossadegh was overthrown, sentenced to three years in prison followed by house arrest for life. The United States had grown from a democratic state under Thomas Jefferson to an imperialist Empire over throwing freely elected governments for the purpose of seizing a small country natural resources in this case their oil. In 2003 President George W. Bush invading the small country of Iraq for the purpose of seizing their natural resources their oil. The Anglo-Iranian Oil company (British Petroleum, BP) arrived in Iran in the early part of the twentieth century. It soon struck the largest oil well that had ever been found in the world. And for the next half-century, it pumped out hundreds of millions of dollars worth of oil from Iran. Great Britain held this monopoly over a poor country and it's poor native people. The British used the Iran oil to build their empire on the backs of third world poor brown people.

The United States after the First World War became the new World Empire and replaced their White British cousins as the new world white imperialist empire.

The Iranian people in 1979 seized the United States Embassy in Iran because of the coup by CIA and British Anglo-Iranian Oil company (British Petroleum) in 1953.The elected Democratic government of Mohammad Mossadegh was overthrown by the United States and The British Petroleum Company BP.

President Baraka Obama made a presidential visit to Israel and the Palestinian 's territory in an attempt to arrange a peace agreement between the Israel and the Palestinian Authority President Obama inherited U.S history of oppression of people of Third World (Black and Brown people).

THE BALFOUR DECLARATION OF 1917

The Balfour Declaration was made in November 1917. The Balfour Declaration promised Jewish communities In Britain and America that Great Britain would support the creation of a Jewish state in Palestine.

On November 2nd 1917, Arthur James Balfour, the British Foreign Secretary wrote to Lord Rothschild that England would support the creation of a Jewish State in Palestine.

The Rothschild's were considered by many Jews to be the most influential of all Jewish families. They were one of the wealthiest families. The Rothschild were the most influential family in Britain and America. Balfour declared his support for the establishment of a Jewish homeland in the land of Palestine. The Rothschild had to obtain Jewish support for Britain and its allies efforts in the First World War. The Jews in countries that were at war against Germany would ensure that Britain won the war against Germany and her allies which were Turkey then the Ottoman Empire (Palestine part of the Ottoman empire). The Ottoman empire was an ally of Germany during the First World

VOTE FOR
Deshay D. Ford

Oxnard Harbor
Commissioner Candidate

- ◆ *EXPERIENCED*
- ◆ *FAIR*
- ◆ *HONEST*

The author at 4 years old.

To
Aunt Edythe &
Uncle Landus
from

Author's dearest Jim Ito
J. Paul Getty Museum, 1990

The author's mother at 35 years old, 1950

In Loving Memory

of the late

Robert Lewis Ford

Services Held:
Saturday, October 8, 1994
11:00 A.M.

Antioch Full Gospel Baptist Church
3824 Antioch Boulevard
College Station, Arkansas -72206

Bishop Kenneth L. Robinson
Pastor----Officiating

Author's beloved brother, Robert Lewis Ford, 1994

In
Celebration of
the Life of

Kamala Gillette

Sunrise:	Sunset:
April 7, 1950	July 25, 2011

Memorial Services
August 9, 2011 at 11:00 AM
East Bay Church of Religious Science
4130 Telegraph Avenue at 41st Street
Oakland, California 94609

Officiating: Reverend Elouise Oliver

Author's dearest cousin, Kamala Gillette, 2011

WHEN ALL IS DONE

When all is done, and my last word is said,
And ye who loved me murmur, "She is dead",
Let no one weep, for fear that I should know,
And sorrow too that ye should sorrow so
When all is done, say not my day is o'er
And that thro' night I seek a dimmer shore:
Say rather that my morn has just begun,
I greet the dawn and not a setting sun,
When all is done.

Paul Laurence Dunbar

Celebrating March Birthdays, 2009
Seated: Garland, Maxwell, Gerri, Edythe, Gladys, Alvin
Standing: Bertram, Frankie,Carl,Carol,Deborah,Antoine,
Linda,Debbi,Braderdine,Sandra,Shani,Harold,Juanita,Kama

Author's Great Aunt, Edythe, celebrating her 90th birthday, 2009

Dr. Ford's sister, Jacquiline Ford Jackson, marriage, 1993
Great Aunt Edythe

Dr. Ford with mother-in-law and Great Aunt Edythe, second mother Eliza-beth, mother-in-law Nellie Hudson, and Rachele Hudson Ford, 1992

Former Consul-general, LR Lawyer, Dies at 78

Graham Roots Hall, aged 78, of 2203 Pine Valley Road, a lawyer and former high-ranking Foreign Service officer, died Thursday.

He had served 10 years in the Foreign Service and was consul-general in Melbourne, Australia, when he retired in 1960.

He also had been counselor and special assistant to the United States ambassador in New Delhi, India, in 1957; special assistant to the assistant secretary of State for United Nations Affairs, and had worked for the United Nations Korean Reconstruction Agency, which was charged with the economic reconstruction of the country after the Korean war. He also held a presidential appointment as delegate to the United Nations Korean Reconstruction Agency.

Practiced Law in LR

After leaving the Foreign Service, he returned to the private practice of law in Little Rock. He had been general counsel to the state Republican Party.

Mr. Hall was born in Little Rock, son of Mr. and Mrs. Walter Graham Hall, and was the third generation of his family to live in Little Rock. His father was cotton broker and real estate investor and his family held stock in the Boyle Realty Company, which owned the Hall and Boyle Buildings. Mr. Hall's grandfather, Milton Guy Hall, was a former mayor of Little Rock, and another grandfather, Maj. P. K. Roots, joined with his brother Col. Logan H. Roots to help establish one of the first public school systems in Arkansas in Fort Smith shortly after the Civil War.

— Staff Photo

GRAHAM ROOTS HALL

Joined Army in 1942

He attended Little Rock public schools, Phillips Exeter Academy, Yale University and the Harvard Law School. He practiced law in Little Rock from 1927 to 1942, when he joined the Army's Judge Advocate General Corps as a captain. He won a commendation for researching and writing an opinion authorizing the lowering of the enlistment age and also served as assistant judge advocate general of the Persian Gulf Command.

In 1944, he was transferred to London and became chairman of the planning and drafting committee of the European Advisory Commission, which was preparing terms for the surrender of Germany and directives concerning the division of powers among Great Britain, the United States and the Soviet Union in occupied Germany. He received the Legion of Merit for this work.

He subsequently was deputy director of restitutions, reparations and deliveries in the United States zone of occupation in Ger-

and returned to Little Rock to practice with the law firm of Moore, Burrow, Chowning and Hall, but was called to active duty in the Korean war. He then entered the State Department after six months' military service.

Before joining the State Department, Mr. Hall had been a member of the Boards of Little Rock Junior College, Dunbar Junior College and Philander Smith College. He also had been a Little Rock School Board member. He was chairman of the Little Rock Committee of the Council on Foreign Relations, a YMCA Board member and chairman of the Board of Stewards of First United Methodist Church.

He and his wife also established the first nursery school and kindergarten in Little Rock and, with Mrs. Ed Cornish, started the first planned parenthood clinic.

Supported College

Mr. Hall, along with his wife, was a long-time supporter of Hendrix College in Conway and had served on its Board of Trustees. Mr. and Mrs. Hall made the largest single contribution to a $1 million Hendrix fund drive in the 1940s and in 1959, he and his wife donated $100,000 in honor of Mrs. Hall's parents, Bishop and Mrs. Herman A. Boaz.

He had been a member of the Administrative Board for Aldersgate Camp, vice president and director of policy for Arkansas for the American Association for the United Nations, chairman of the International Hospitality Committee of Pulaski County, member of the Board of Directors of the United Fund and chairman of the County Appeals Review Board.

He was a member of the Rotary Club of Little Rock, the Kiwanis Club, the Country Club of Little Rock, the Little Rock, the Yale Club and the Harvard Law School Association.

Survivors are his wife, Ruth Boaz Hall; two sons, Lee Boaz Hall of Chicago and Donald Hall of Tucson, Ari., and grandchildren.

A memorial service will be at p.m. Saturday at Trinity Episcopal Cathedral by Very Rev. W. Pugh, Rev. Alvin C. and Rev. Robert E. L. Bearden. Arrangements are by Ruebel Funeral Home. Memorials may be made to Hendrix College in some way or a favorite charity.

Graham & Louise Halll, 1954-1957 Consul-General to India and Australia, U.S. State Department

Mrs. Louise Boaz Hall, LR civic leader, dies

Helped organize Birth Control Clinic

Mrs. Louise Boaz Hall, aged 82, one of the founders of the organization that is now the Planned Parenthood Association of Arkansas, died Thursday at Tucson.

She was the widow of Col. Graham Roots Hall, a lawyer and Foreign Service diplomat.

Mrs. Hall was born at Fort Worth, the daughter of Methodist Bishop Hiram A. Boaz, co-founder of Southern Methodist University and for several years Methodist bishop of Arkansas. She had traveled extensively with her parents to China, Korea and Japan, where her father also served as bishop. She graduated from Barnard College in 1925.

After her marriage in 1927, Mr. and Mrs. Hall settled at Little Rock, where she became active in community affairs.

Mrs. Hall helped organize the Birth Control Clinic of Arkansas, now the Planned Parenthood Association. She also helped found the Visiting Nurses Association of Little Rock and became that organization's first president. She is credited with establishing the first nursery school in Arkansas.

She served as president of the Junior League of Little Rock and, on behalf of that organization, helped organize the Family Service Agency of Little Rock. She was Family Service's first vice president and only female board member.

Mrs. Hall served on the executive committee of the Council of Social Agencies and the Community Chest, served as delegate to several national conferences of the Association of Junior Leagues of America and was chairman of the regional nominating committee of the League.

During World War II, Mrs. Hall helped organize and served as first vice president of the Volunteer Bureau of Arkansas and served as president of the Central Volunteer Bureau of Little Rock.

From 1942 to 1945 Mrs. Hall was acting president of the Dixie Bauxite Company and acting executive vice president of the Boyle Realty Company.

Mrs. Hall and her husband moved to Washington, D.C., in 1951 where Colonel Hall served as an official of the United Nations Korean Reconstruction Agency. During that time, Mrs. Hall was deputy director of the Office of Volunteers at the American Red Cross. For her work she received the first certificate of merit given to a volunteer by the national Red Cross headquarters.

While at Washington, Mrs. Hall was secretary of the Dumbarton House Board of the Colonial Dames of America national headquarters.

From 1955 to 1957, while Mrs. Hall's husband was special assistant to the United States ambassador at New Delhi, she was art editor of the American women's newspaper. When her husband was assigned as consul general to Melbourne, Australia, in 1957, Mrs. Hall was patroness of the American Women's Auxiliary to the Royal Children's Hospital of Melbourne.

After her husband retired from the Foreign Service in 1961, the Halls returned to Little Rock and built their home, Pine Knoll.

Mrs. Hall was a life-long Methodist and a member of the First United Methodist Church of Little Rock, a former president and vice president of the Little Rock Garden Club, a member of the Arkansas Arts Center, Little Rock Country Club and the Belgrave Club of Washington.

She and her husband were yachting enthusiasts and had cruised the inland waterway system, the Great Lakes and the St. Lawrence Seaway.

Survivors are two sons, Lee Boaz Hall of Chicago and Donald Roots Hall of Tucson, and six grandchildren.

Arrangements will be announced by Ruebel Funeral Home.

Memorials may be made to Planned Parenthood of Little Rock or the Memorial Medical Center at Ludington, Mich.

Win Rockefeller: lawmaker

Billionaire politician member of famous family

By Kelly P. Kissel
The Associated Press

LITTLE ROCK, Ark. — Lt. Gov. Win Rockefeller, the unassuming billionaire who last year abandoned a race for Arkansas governor — a post once held by his father — died Sunday after unsuccessful treatments for a blood disorder, his office said. He was 57.

Rockefeller died Sunday morning at the University of Arkansas for Medical Sciences with his family present, his spokesman Steve Brawner said.

Bone marrow transplants Oct. 7 and March 29 at Seattle's Fred Hutchinson Cancer Center failed to cure an unclassified myeloproliferative disorder. He returned to Arkansas on July 8 and immediately entered the hospital. The next day, Rockefeller notified Gov. Mike Huckabee that he could not continue his duties, at least temporarily.

"Win Rockefeller embodied the ideals of compassion, generosity, and humility. He was a wealthy man, but his real wealth was not his money, but his heart for serving others," Huckabee said in a statement.

Under the Arkansas constitution, Huckabee does not have the authority to name a replacement to fill the remainder of Rockefeller's term, which ends in January. Senate President Jim Argue, D-Little Rock, will direct Arkansas government when Huckabee is out of state.

The great-grandson of Standard Oil founder John D. Rockefeller ranked No. 283 on the Forbes magazine list of the nation's wealthiest people in 2005, with a fortune the magazine estimated at $1.2 billion. As lieutenant governor, a part-time job, he donated his $34,673 state salary to charity.

Rockefeller was the only child of former Gov. Winthrop Rockefeller and Barbara "Bobo" Sears. An uncle was former vice president Nelson Rockefeller. Win entered politics in 1996, winning a special election to complete the unexpired lieutenant governor term of Huckabee.

Rockefeller won re-election twice. As lieutenant governor, he presided over the state Senate and served as governor when Huckabee was out of the state.

He also served as an economic cheerleader for the state, traveling at his own expense to seek foreign investments here.

Under the state's term-limits law, he could not serve another term.

Huckabee and Rockefeller had an amiable relationship. The governor appeared to brand Rockefeller as his heir apparent in 2004 when he said voters should vote a GOP ticket in 2006.

Rockefeller was a member of the Arkansas State Police Commission from 1981 to 1995 and chairman of the President's Council on Rural America after his appointment in 1991 by the first President Bush.

Two of his eight children have Down syndrome, and Rockefeller and his second wife, Lisenne, started what is now the Academy at Riverdale, a school for children with learning disabilities.

Survivors include his second wife, his mother, three daughters, five sons, a granddaughter, a stepbrother and a stepsister.

ROCKEFELLER

Author met Rockefeller at Graham Hall's home. Little Rock, Ark, 1980

26. A warm greeting by an old family friend: The Premier says goodbye to the author following their midnight-to-3:00 A.M. visit in Peking shortly before President Nixon's historic trip to China in 1972.

27. "Mrs. Mansfield and I may well have been the last Americans to see the late Premier. We visited him in his hospital room in late December, 1974, and spent over an hour with him . . . He accompanied us as we prepared to say farewell, and then spoke these final words: 'The door between our two countries should never have been closed.'"

MY DEAR FRIEND John McCook Roots
MEETING CHOU EN LAI 1972

Former State Department Consul-General to India and Australia, 1956
My mentor Dr. Grahaam Rootss Hall, 1978, Little Rock Ark.

MEMORIAL
AND
COMMITTAL
SERVICE

Lee Boaz Hall

October 8, 1928
Little Rock, Arkansas

January 18, 2004
Summerland, California

Sarah

Lee finished his work on earth and left the stage in a
manner that leaves those of us left behind with a cry of
agony in our hearts: As the fragile thread of our faith is
dealt with so violently. Are any of us strong enough to
stay conscious through such teaching as we are
receiving? Probably very few: And even they would
only have a whisper of equanimity and spacious peace
amid the screaming trumpets of their rage, grief and
desolation? I can't assuage our pain with any words--
nor should I--for our pain is Lee's legacy to all of us:

Author's dearest friend, Lee Boaz Hall, 2004,
Graham and Louise Hall, older son

My great dear devoted and love friend, Louise Boaz Hall and Danny Haye and friend. Australia, 1956

JABS &
STRAIGHT
WRITES

THE X FACTOR

A RARE CASSIUS CLAY SIGNATURE WOULD FETCH A HEFTY SUM

"The Greatest" has signed a lot of autographs, first as Cassius Clay and, for the past half century, as Muhammad Ali. If one estimates that he signed 50 signatures a day for much of his adult life, that would equal almost a million signatures.

But one signature is particularly rare.

Clay defeated Sonny Liston to claim the heavyweight championship on Feb. 25, 1964. Two days later, he told the media

This man signed a name other than Cassius Clay or Muhammad Ali for a short time.

Farewell to Manzanar

Jeanne Wakatsuki Houston
and James D. Houston

To My FRIEND
DESHAY AT THE
AMERICAN RED CROSS
1 - 14 -10

to the memory of

Ko and Riku Wakatsuki

and Woodrow M. Wakatsuki

Patricia M. Wakatsuki Kosmo

THE AUTHOR'S DEAR FRIEND
PATRICIA KOSMO (WAKATSUKI)

PATRICIA WAS
4 YEARS OLD WHEN
SHE AND HER WAS
ROUNDED UP IN 1941
AND PLACE INTO
U.S. CONCENTRATION
CAMP "FAREWELL
TO MANZANAR
LOVE ALWAYS REMEMBER
DEAR, I WILL UNTIL GOD CALL
YOU HOME
Amen

DURING WORLD WAR TWO A COMMUNITY called Manzanar was hastily created in the high mountain desert country of California, east of the Sierras. Its purpose was to house thousands of Japanese Americans. One of the first families to arrive was the Wakatsukis, who were ordered to leave their fishing business in Long Beach and take with them only the belongings they could carry. For Jeanne Wakatsuki, a seven-year-old child, Manzanar became a way of life in which she struggled and adapted, observed and grew. For her father it was essentially the end of his life.

At age thirty-seven, Jeanne Wakatsuki Houston recalls life at Manzanar through the eyes of the child she was. She tells of her fear, confusion, and bewilderment as well as the dignity and great resourcefulness of people in oppressive and demeaning circumstances. Written with her husband, Jeanne delivers a powerful first-person account that reveals her search for the meaning of Manzanar.

First published in 1973, this reissue of the classic memoir of a devastating Japanese American experience now includes an inspiring afterword by the authors.

When I saw him again a few days after the Liston fight, he was very different—and very serious. He was on his way to a Muslim rally; that's why he was wearing the bow tie. He wasn't joking and kidding around the way he used to.

Author met Ali at college, 1970

CHOU

An Informal Biography
of China's Legendary
CHOU EN-LAI

John McCook Roots

CHOU

John McCook Roots

John Roots, an American newspaper-man who grew up in China, has written an informal biography of a man who was his friend, China's late Premier, Chou En-lai. To understand China, says Roots, one must begin by under-standing this man, who was Premier of the Chinese People's Republic from its inception in 1949 and was its voice to the world for a quarter of a century.

Chou survived five civil wars, two world wars, a dozen years of Japanese aggression, a decade of Soviet hostility, and two decades of United States ostra-cism to become the most durable and resilient political figure of our age. Here, John McCook Roots follows Chou throughout his incredible life—one of unparalleled drama and self-sacrifice. The book, however, is more than a biography. It is also a memoir, a recollection of Roots' own childhood in China, when he witnessed firsthand

(continued on back flap)

John Roots was cousin of Dr. Graham R. Hall.

26. A warm greeting by an old family friend: The Premier says good-bye to the author following their midnight-to-3:00 A.M. visit in Peking shortly before President Nixon's historic trip to China in 1972.

27. "Mrs. Mansfield and I may well have been the last Americans to see the late Premier. We visited him in his hospital room in late December 1974, and spent over an hour with him . . . He accompanied us as we prepared to say farewell, and then spoke these final words: 'The door between our two countries should never have been closed.'"

MY DEAR FRIEND John Mcade Roots
meeting CHOU Em hAi 1972

My dear friend Judith Roots meeting Chou Em Lai, 1972

CHOU

John McCook Roots

John Roots, an American newspaper-man who grew up in China, has written an informal biography of a man who was his friend, China's late Premier, Chou En-lai. To understand China, says Roots, one must begin by under-standing this man, who was Premier of the Chinese People's Republic from its inception in 1949 and was its voice to the world for a quarter of a century.

Chou survived five civil wars, two world wars, a dozen years of Japanese aggression, a decade of Soviet hostility, and two decades of United States ostra-cism to become the most durable and resilient political figure of our age. Here, John McCook Roots follows Chou throughout his incredible life—one of unparalleled drama and self-sacrifice. The book, however, is more than a biography. It is also a memoir, a recollection of Roots' own childhood in China, when he witnessed firsthand

(continued on back flap)

John Roots was cousin of Dr. Graham R. Hall.

With all Good Wishes

for

Christmas and the New Year

from

The Administrator and Lady Burbury

Author met Sir Staney and Lady Burbury, 1978,
at Graham Hall's Home, Little Rock, Ark

18. After the Sino-Indian border war of 1959–60, precipitated by the Dalai Lama's flight from Tibet, Chou and his new Foreign Minister Ch'en Yi (extreme right) conferred seven times with Nehru in New Delhi. This time the two friends failed to agree and shortly afterward Nehru died, a bitter enemy of Peking.

19. Following Stalin's death, relations between Peking and Moscow rapidly deteriorated. The climax came with Chou's 1961 Moscow visit when Peking openly challenged the Kremlin for leadership of the Communist world. On his return, Chou was given a hero's welcome by Mao.

Chou Em-Lai was a good friend of Mr. Root's father.

16. Prince (later King) Feisal of Saudi Arabia meets Chou at the Bandung Conference in Indonesia (April 1955). This began Communist China's concerted diplomatic activity throughout Asia, Africa and the Middle East.

17. China's Chou and Vietnam's Ho Chi-minh, the two most widely traveled leaders of the Communist world, renew their friendship in Peking after Bandung.

Legendary Vietnam Gen. Giap, 102, dies

By Chris Brummitt
Associated Press

HANOI, Vietnam — Gen. Vo Nguyen Giap, the brilliant and ruthless commander who led a ragtag army of guerrillas to victory in Vietnam over first the French and then the Americans, died Friday. The last of the country's old-guard revolutionaries was 102.

A national hero, Giap enjoyed a legacy second only to that of his mentor, independence leader Ho Chi Minh.

Giap died in a military hospital in the capital of Hanoi, where he had spent nearly four years because of illnesses, according to a government official and a person close to him. Both spoke on condition of anonymity before the death was announced in state-controlled media.

Known as the "Red Napoleon," Giap commanded guerrillas who wore sandals made of car tires and lugged artillery piece by piece over mountains to encircle and crush the French army at Dien Bien Phu in 1954. The unlikely victory — still studied at military schools — led to Vietnam's independence and hastened the collapse of colonialism across Indochina and beyond.

Giap then defeated the U.S.-backed South Vietnam government in 1975, reuniting a country that had been split into communist and noncommunist states. He regularly accepted heavy combat losses to achieve his goals.

"No other wars for national liberation were as fierce or caused as many losses as this war," Giap said in 2005.

"But we still fought because for Vietnam, nothing is more precious than independence and freedom," he said, repeating a famous quote by Ho Chi Minh.

Although widely revered in Vietnam, Giap was the nemesis of millions of South Vietnamese who fought alongside U.S. troops and fled their homeland after the war.

Late in life, Giap encouraged warmer relations between Vietnam and the U.S., which re-established ties in 1995 and have become close trading partners. Vietnam has also recently looked to the U.S. military as a way to balance China's growing power in the disputed South China Sea.

"We can put the past behind," Giap said in 2000. "But we cannot completely forget it."

Former Defense Secretary Robert McNamara (left) speaks to onetime foe Gen. Vo Nguyen Giap in 1997. Officials say Giap, who drove the French and the Americans out of Vietnam, died Friday.

John Roots was in Firearm Tournament in Asia, 1978, Little Rock Arkansas

COOPER, John Sherman, (1901 - 1991)

Senate Years of Service: 1946-1949; 1952-1955; 1956-1973
Party: Republican; Republican; Republican

COOPER, John Sherman, a Senator from Kentucky; born in Somerset, Pulaski County, Ky., August 23, 1901; attended the public schools at Somerset and Centre College, Danville, Ky.; graduated from Yale College 1923; attended Harvard Law School 1923-1925; admitted to the bar in 1928 and commenced practice in Somerset, Ky.; member, Kentucky house of representatives 1928-1930; judge of Pulaski County, Ky., 1930-1938; member of the board of trustees of the University of Kentucky 1935-1946; served during the Second World War in the United States Army 1942-1946, attaining the rank of captain; elected circuit judge of the twenty-eighth judicial district of Kentucky in 1945 and served until his resignation in November 1946; elected on November 5, 1946, as a Republican to the United States Senate to fill the vacancy caused by the resignation of Albert B. Chandler and served from November 6, 1946, to January 3, 1949; unsuccessful candidate for reelection in 1948; resumed the practice of law; delegate to the General Assembly of the United Nations in 1949 and alternate delegate in 1950 and 1951; served as adviser to the Secretary of State at the London and Brussels meetings of the Council of Ministers of the North Atlantic Treaty Organization in 1950; elected on November 4, 1952, as a Republican to the United States Senate to fill the vacancy caused by the death of Virgil M. Chapman and served from November 5, 1952, to January 3, 1955; unsuccessful candidate for reelection in 1954; Ambassador to India and Nepal 1955-1956; delegate, United Nations General Assembly 1968; elected on November 6, 1956, as a Republican to the United States Senate to fill the vacancy caused by the death of Alben W. Barkley; reelected in 1960, and again in 1966, and served from November 7, 1956, to January 3, 1973; was not a candidate for reelection in 1972; Ambassador to the German Democratic Republic 1974-1976; resumed the practice of law in Washington, D.C., and was a resident of Somerset, Ky., and Washington, D.C., until his death in Washington, D.C., February 21, 1991; interment in Arlington National Cemetery, Arlington, Va.

Author met John Sherman Cooper in 1977 at the home of Graham Hall, Little Rock, Ark

Hugh Thompson, Jr.

From Wikipedia, the free encyclopedia

Hugh Clowers Thompson, Jr. (April 15, 1943 – January 6, 2006) was a United States Army helicopter pilot during the Vietnam War. He is best known for his role in stopping the My Lai Massacre, in which a group of US Army soldiers tortured and killed several hundred unarmed Vietnamese civilians, mutilating their bodies after they had been murdered. Although initially ill-treated in some quarters for their intervention, Thompson and his crew, Glenn Andreotta and Lawrence Colburn, were recognized and decorated many years later for their heroism at My Lai. Andreotta had died in combat three weeks after the massacre, and so was honored posthumously.

Hugh Clowers Thompson, Jr.

Contents

Early life

Hugh Clowers Thompson, Jr. was born on April 15, 1943, in Atlanta, Georgia.[1] He grew up in rural Stone Mountain, Georgia, raised by his strict parents. [2][3] After dropping out of Troy State University, he volunteered for the United States Navy in 1961 and served with a Seabee construction unit from 1961 to 1964. After this, he returned home to Georgia and ran a funeral home.

Born	April 15, 1943 Atlanta, Georgia, United S
Died	January 6, 2006 (aged 62) Pineville, Louisiana, Unit(States
Place of burial	Lafayette, Louisiana, Uni States
Allegiance	United States of Am
Service/branch	United States Navy United States Army
Years of service	1961–1964 (Navy), 196((Army)
Rank	Major
Unit	Seabees 161st Aviation Compar (Assault Helicopter)

I admired this remarkable human being, Dr. Ford, 1991

Sir Winston Churchill in Jamaica, 1953. "What would Michael say about all this?"

Author met Hugh Foot in 1969. He was British Ambaassador
of United Nations at Graham Hall Home, Little Rock, Ark

War. Balfour promised the Jews that they could have Palestine as a Jewish Home Land for their support of the British's war efforts. The British promised the Arabs the same lands for their support against the Germans and the Ottoman Empire. The Jews in Germany and Austria sabotage the German's war efforts and their reward from United Kingdom was the land of Palestine (Israel).

Therefore, while Britain was given Palestine to govern as a league of nations at the end of the first World War. The Jews and the Arabs both claimed Palestine as their land. The United States begin supporting the Jews because of the power of the American Jews and because of the belief in the concept of White Man burden which was the primary philosophy of the United States government and of the American public.

The United States had moved from democratic Republic under Thomas Jefferson 1800 to Empire after the first and Second World Wars. The United States like their cousins the British had begin as a small geographic area in Britain to a World Empire and United States as thirteen colonies to an empire for seizing and conquering their neighbors (Britain Wale, Ireland, Scotland) the United States through the War of 1846-1848 with Mexico and the seizure of Indians Lands through the Indian Wars had become an Empire built by slave labor. The White House and Washington Mall was built by slave labor. Great Britain utilized the slave labor of their India Colony in British India to provide the back breaking labor for building the British empire.

THE CIA COUP IN CHILE IN 1973 DESTROYED
THE U. S IMAGE AS A SUPPORTER OF DEMOCRACY

September 11 is now imprinted on the history of America. Yet for the South American Country of Chile, the date has a different and much more tragic significance. It was on that day in 1973 that the democratically-elected government of Salvador Allende was overthrown in a CIA-backed military coup. Augusto Pinochet seized power. In the ensuring years ten of thousands of Chileans were killed, jailed, tortured and driven into exile. The U.S. role, under Nixon and his national Security Advisor Henry Kissinger, at first destabilizing and then overthrowing the Allende government was Decisive. It will rank among the most inhumane interventions ever undertaken by the US. A few years after the coup, Nobel Peace Prize-winner Kissinger visited Chile. He told General Pinochet, in the United States, as you know, we are sympathetic with what you are trying to do here. The U.S. supported and encouraged the killing and torturing of Chilean citizens.

Henry Kissinger is currently wanted in European World Court for War Crime. George W. bush is also wanted by the European World Court for War crimes. George W. Bush invaded Iraq without being attacked in clear violation of the United Nation Charter of being an aggressor country. Adolph Hitler's Generals were put on trial in the World Court for invading a peaceful countries which had not threatened nor initiated any military aggression toward Germany (March,2003-2013). Salvador Allende was a social democrat, very much of the European type. He called for minor redistribution of wealth, to help the poor (Chile had an unfair society). The CIA had spend a great deal of American Taxpayers money to see that Chile was not a democratic society. Allende was a doctor, and one of the things he did was to institute a free milk program for half a million very poor, malnourished children. He called for nationalization of a major industries like cooper mining, and for a policy on international independence-meaning that Chile would not simply subordinate itself to the US, but would take more of an independent path. The CIA with the approval of Henry Kissinger and President Richard Nixon gave the approval to overthrow the democratic election government of Salvador Allende in 1973. Henry Kissinger and Richard Nixon pulled out the stops on the over throw of Allende on September 11, 1973 (President had given the CIA, Willie Roosevelt, CIA station chief in Iran to over throw Mohammad Mossadegh, 1953). The United States Empire like their cousin the British Empire motive in the Opium War was (1839-1842) the making of money on the suffering of poor people of the Third World. When the CIA over threw the Government of Allende the CIA placed General Augusto Pinochet in power. CIA placing Pinochet in power ensured years of thousand of Chileans were killed, jailed, tortured, and driven into exile. The US role under Nixon and his National Security Advisor Henry Kissinger, in first destabilizing and the over throwing the Allende government was decisive.

The United States used the CIA to over thrown democratic elected governments all over the world for half a century. The United States white colonists begin a race campaign to destroy the native people of the North American continent for the purpose of seizing their lands and destroying their race and culture (1838-1892). President Andrew Jackson removing the Cherokee nation in the Trial of Tearing 1836 and the final battle at Wound Knee in 1892 ended the frontier with the racial genocide of native people.

THE DESTRUCTION OF THE ROMAN EMPIRE

The Rome Empire begin with Augustus 27 B.C to 476 A.D with the last Roman Emperor Romulus Augustus in 476 A.D. Rome like the American Empire begin as a Republic in 507 B.C. The American Empire begin with the founding of the little American Republic in 1787 with the Signing of the American Constitution in Philadelphia. Augustus realized after the murder of his Uncle Julius Caesar in 44 B.C. he could not appear to be a dictator and seize power from the Roman's citizens. Augustus did not want to be assassinated like his Uncle. Augustus formed a Republican Government with himself as the head of government for life (monarchy government). Rome had acquired a vast number of cities and cultures and people that the military had conquered. Augustus became head of government for life and the Roman's Senate pass a decree that made Augustus an Emperor (In fact Rome had become an Empire). A democratic government cannot govern an Empire. An empire need one person at the top making all of the decisions and laws for a vast majority of people and countries the empire has conquered. The Roman's Empire begin with the honorable Augustus being named as the Emperor. The roman's Senate declared Augustus a God to be worshipped by the people of the Empire. The British Empire had made Queen Victoria the Empress of the British Empire. The people of the British Empire could look to Queen Victoria as their mother as well as queen.

The American Empire begin with Abraham Lincoln prosecuting the Civil War as a police action not as a declared war by the United States Senate. President fought the entire Civil War as the Commanding Chief of American military. President Lincoln's action during the Civil War allowed President Lyndon B. Johnson to fight the Vietnam War as a police Action. President Thurman committed American troops to the Korean War without congress declaring war and Johnson the Vietnam War in 1965.

The Roman Empire begin by conquering it's neighbors and acquiring their natural resources. In 46 A.D the Roman's Army under Claudius Caesar conquered the British Isles. The Roman conquered England and made the English slaves and they established military outposts. The British once establishing their Empire conquered the country of India and made their inhabitants slaves (1795 Clive defeated the Indians and made India a colony of Britain).

The American Colonists obtained their independence from England and begin the process of conquering the native populations and seizing their natural resources and their lands. The American Colonists obtained their independence in 1781 with the Treaty of Paris which ended the American Revolutionary War. New American Republic begin their wars with the native populations killing the native people and seizing their lands. The United States also militarily seized territories from Mexico, California, Arizona, New Mexico, Colorado and other territory through the Mexican American War from 1846-1848. The United States further utilized slave's labor to build the White House 1791-1815(burned down by the British in The War of 1812). The American White House where the family of Baraka Obama was built by utilizing the labor of slaves brought and purchased from Africa slave merchants. The Jewish people were the major slave merchants and they made a great deal of money out of buying and selling black African people. During the American Civil War Jewish Southerners fought for the confederate Cause. Rome begin as a small city in Italy. This original settlement grew to a large city. Rome was founded in 753 B.C. The young American colonies had similar beginning. The first American Colony begin in Virginia (The name Virginia came from Queen Elizabeth the Virgin Queen 1607). By alliances with surrounding communities and through a long succession of wars against the Etruscans in the north and other tribes in the south Rome became master of the Italian Peninsula by 265 B.C. The American colonists became the masters of the East and part of the west by killing and taking Native Americans' land by seizure, treaties, and military conquest. The Roman had aristocratic families. They were the families of Gaius Julius Caesar and the of Tiberius Claudius Drusus the Julio-Claudian Emperors ruled Rome for 90 years. The United states had their royal families. They were the Washington, the Jefferson, the Roosevelt, the Rockefeller, the Bush, the Clinton and last the

Obama's. The American royal families ruled through their connections at Yale, Harvard, and Princeton (President Obama and Mrs. Obama both graduated from the Harvard Law School).

Rome begin by conquering their neighbors the Etruscans and the Carthaginians on their way to building an empire. The American colonists begin by conquering the native people(Indians Wars, 1862-1892 De Brown Bury my Heart At Wounded Knee 1892) and seizing their lands. The US seized Mexican's lands in the War of 1846-1848.

The Roman controlled the entire Mediterranean for nearly 500 hundred years. In 60 B.C

Pompey conquered the Middle East. Rome 's agricultural changed from being producers to a civilization of consumers. The Roman conquered the middle East which became the bread basket for the Roman empire. The Empire needed the farmers of the Middle East to produce all of the food and other good consumed by the Roman citizen in the city of Rome. When the Jews rebelled in 68 A.D. the Roman Emperor Nero brought the Roman Army from Britain to put down the rebellion of their sources of food and other goods of consumption. In 2001 George Herbert Walter Bush had to put down the army of Iraq's army invasion of Kuwait in 2000. Iraq was attempting to control American food supply (Iraq Oil supply). In 2003 George W. Bush the son of G.HW Bush invaded Iraq to prevent the country of Iraq from controlling American food supply the Oil of the world coming out of the Middle East.

WHY DID THE ROMAN EMPIRE COLLAPSE

The Roman Empire begin to decline after the Augustus Caesar became the emperor of the Empire. Augustus expanded the Empire through military conquest. After Augustus defeated Anthony In 31 B.C. the army was private soldiers in the employment of the general who could pay their salaries. The original Roman's army was citizen soldiers who served during time of military Emergency. After 31 B.C the army became a professional army that was loyal to the Augustus 's Family. Augustus paid the army and they owned total loyalty to the Emperor.

Augustus making the Roman's Army into a professional army led to the decline of the state. The Romans begin the process of recruiting soldiers from the conquered population the Germanic tribes. The people in Roman begin to be corrupted by materialism, homosexual behavior by Roman's males. The Roman begin to recruit Germans to fight Germans because the Romans' males were very homosexual. The Roman's army had become an army of German conquered people. The Romans had to used Germans to fight German people.

During the George W. Bush's war against Iraq the majority of the soldiers were non-white soldiers from the conquered groups, African-Americans and Latino soldiers. I had to go to Los Angeles on 12/27/2011 to the United States federal court building. In the Federal court building In the hall way were all of the American soldiers killed in Iraq during the year of 2011. The majority of the soldiers killed from California were Latino soldiers. The ancient Roman empire used their conquered German Populations as soldiers. The United States empire were using Latino and African-American young people as soldiers of the American Empire.

President George W. Bush did not require his nephew George W. Bush the fourth to serve in Iraq. Nor did President Bush's daughters served in the United State Army. Republican President candidate Mitt Romney 's five sons did not served in the United State Army in the Iraq's war. The Iraq War was fought with the racially oppressed minorities and economic poor white people. Augustus begin to employ the conquered German as soldiers as a result of not enough healthy and strong Italians as soldiers. A Roman's army under Publius Quinctilius Varus a cousin of Augustus in A.D 9 was defeated in the Teutoburg Forest by Arminius a former Germanic general who had once served in the roman's Army (The Romans From Village to Empire, Mary T. Boatwright, Daniel J. Gargola, and Richard J.A. Talbert, New York,2004). The Rome had spread beyond what the treasury could paid to maintain. The United States has reached a point wherefore the American Empire cannot afford and Empire (maintain troops in the Korean peninsula, 1950-2013).

In its heyday the Roman army was composed of citizens and subjects. Legionaries were recruited from subject states (conquered people Germany Tribes). The Romans recruited the Germans, though they had a racial prejudice of the German race. The United States army recruit blacks and Latino they have also a racial hatred of brown and black people (racial toward Brown immigrants). The transition from a citizen's army to a very nearly mercenary one did not go smoothly. The Germans who were admired for their military prowess were also the enemy. In the American Empire the Brown and Black soldiers are seen by the white majority as the enemy and as criminals, lazy, and welfare recipients. The Roman passed laws to prevent intermarriage between the Roman population and the Germanic population (U.S. prevented marriage between black and white people, Supreme Court over turned the law 1967). Racial prejudice and Xenophobia toward the Germanic people became very dominant in the last century of the Roman Empire. Under president Obama the first American African-American President racial prejudice toward black and brown people have become very dominant in the American Empire of 2013 (Racial prejudice of white Tea party, Presidential election of 2012). Racial profiling of black and Browns males and the killing of Black and Brown males by American cities police departments.

There were many causes of the fall of the Roma's Empire. The Roman's population begin to decrease. The populations of the German tribes were on the increase. In the United States the white population number are on the decline and the non-white population numbers are on the increase (Brown and Asian people, census 2010). The homosexuality of the males of the Roman population. California passed proposition 8 recognizing marriage between a man and woman as legal in California. The 9th Circuit Court found the Proposition 8th to be under constitutional and violated the rights of gay people. The Roman army after a major defeat at Adrianople 378 A.D. could not recover from the major defeat. The United States army defeats in Iraq and Afghanistan cannot maintain the their current commitments. The Roman army could not protect the frontiers from the attacks of the Germanic tribes. The Roman could not raise enough taxes to pay for the army nor the other government commitments. The decrease in loyalty of the upper classes. The major burden of taxes fell on the lower classes. The Rich were avoiding their military obligations. Mitt Romney had five adults sons and not one of his sons ever served in U.S. George W. Bush fought the 2003 War against Iraq with soldiers from the white economic oppress class and the racial oppress groups of African-Americans and the Latinos. George W.

Bush daughters nor nephew served in the U.S. army during George W. Bush's Iraq War (President Trump new tax bill 2017 benefitted men of the rich class not poor U.S. citizens). There was a decline in morals and values in Rome. During the reign of Marcus Aurelius there were 32, 000 prostitutes in Rome. During George W. Bush Presidency there was children prostitution and children sexual molestation and child slavery all over the U.S. Empire (Pen State Child molestation crisis). There was political corruption in the Rome Empire around the selection of new emperors. In the 2012 Presidential elections President Obama and his rival Mitt Romney both spend over a billion dollars during the Presidential election. The Roman Empire had a major problems with unemployment for the masses of their citizens. The Roman's citizen farmer could not compete with the large slave estates owned by the wealth class. The small citizen farmers were forced out of business. The city of Rome was over populated with the poor unemployed. The United States farmers and business people cannot compete with the cheap goods coming from China and other parts of the Developing World. In Rome a large number of people were on government food (oil from the Middle East) and other forms of support. The Roman Empire had to keep a large army in the Middle East to protect their food supply and the US has to keep a large army in the Middle East to protect their oil supply. The US has to protect Israel and the Roman's army had to protect Jerusalem, Syria, Palestine from the Parthian 's Empire. The US. Has to keep a large Army in South Korea to protect their allies from the nuclear power of the North Koreans. The Romans did not have the tax base to provide for such a large military commitment. The United States do not have the tax base to provide for all of their military commitments. The military expenditures were a large drain on the government depleting resources. The United States had to borrow money from China to fight the Iraq War. The Chinese Government and businesses own a major share of the United States economy. The final blow to the Roman Empire was the increase in the number of Germanic tribes attacking the Roman's frontiers. The United States have military threats from the a power nuclear North Korea and a economic and military rising Chinese Empire. The Roman Empire attempted to bring the Goths a Germanic tribe into the Roman's territory as allies. There was racial prejudice from the Roman population against the Goths tribe and exploitation by Roman's merchants of the Goth's populations. The racial prejudice and exploitation led to a war between the Romans and their ally the Goth (Adrianople 378 A.D. battle). At the battle of Adrianople 378 A.D. a Roman Army under the Emperor Valens was defeated by the Goths under their leader Fritigern. The Roman's army nor the Roman Empire never recovered from their defeat at Adrianople 378 A.D. (Adolph Hitler Army never recovered from their defeat at Stalingrad 1943). The United States army never recovered from their defeats by the North Vietnamese in 1975 and the Iraq War of 2003-2012.

The Roman's population was in decline and the populations of the oppressed conquered people the Goths and other Germanic tribes were on the increase. The white populations In the United States is on decrease and the population of the racially oppressed groups in Unites States the Asians, Latinos, Black are on the increase.(U.S. immigration battles). The United States army like the Roman Army had begin to recruit from the Germanic tribes and the US recruit from their racially oppressed groups. The Roman population did not over come their racial prejudice against the Germanic tribes. The United States white population has not overcome their racial prejudice against their people of color (2012 Presidential Election the Republican party candidates racial hate of people of color).

Then in 476 A.D. the Germanic General Odoacer overthrew the last of the Roman Emperor, Augustus Romulus. With the overthrow of Augustus Romulus the Roman Empire in the West came to an end. In the year 331 A.D. the Emperor Diocletian divided up the Roma's world into two halves. The Western Roman Empire and the new Eastern Roman's world with it's capital Nicomdia (modern Turkey). The Eastern Roman Emperor Constantine changed the name of the Eastern Roman Empire to Constantinople in about the 305 A.D. The City of Constantinople lasted for a 1000 years and was conquered by the Ottoman Turks in 1453 A.D.

TRAJAN 98-117 A.D. ROME LAST IMPERIALISTIC EMPEROR

Once Trajan became emperor he begin expanding the Rome's territories. Trajan brought more wealth by his conquest of new territories into the Roman's Empire. In 115, Jewish communities in Cyrenaica rebelled against Roman's authority. Roman could conquer new territories but it could not hold on to these new conquest. Trajan different then the Julio-Claudian Emperors Trajan came from Spanish province. Trajan had always been a soldier in the Roman Army. Roman had become wealthy by conquering other lands and new territories which brought Gold, silver and slaves. The Emperor Hadrian was selected by Trajan as his successor. The Empire shifted from an acquiring empire to a none conquering empire under Hadrian in 117 A.D. Hadrian begin the process of consolidation of the empire not expansion. Hadrian was similar to president Baraka Obama he was of Greek origins. Hadrian was a well educated Emperor and he favored the arts over military conquest and soldiering. Like President Obama he did not favor enlarging the military, but building defensive walls to keep the Germanic tribe s out of Roman's territory. Hadrian favored programs for the poor of Rome and more services. Hadrian worked hard to show that he was approachable and cordial, but with mixed success. President Obama attempted to bring bipartisan cooperation among Democrats and Republicans with little success. Hadrian improve the conditions of slaves by requiring that an owner obtain the approval of a magistrate before killing any slave who had committed a crime. Hadrian improved the conditions of the elderly by providing more services. Hadrian traveled all over the empire and listened to their grievances. The upper classes fought against all of the changes Hadrian were attempting to make as the Roman Emperor. Hadrian made the path to Roman Citizenship easier for the conquered people of the Roman Empire. Hadrian begin the process of ending the campaigns of conquest which was under the Emperor Trajan (President Obama begin the process of reduction of American military forces). President Obama has begun the process of concentrating on Asia not the Middle East. President Obama like the Emperor Hadrian who was of Greek origins and President Obama of African-American culture background. Hadrian built the Hadrian Wall in Great Britain. Hadrian improved the condition of slave class. Hadrian begin a campaign of building and other benefactions throughout the Roman Empire. Hadrian mingle with the people of Rome and the provinces. Hadrian traveled constantly throughout the Empire. Hadrian even traveled to the British Isles. Despite renouncing further expansion, he took a keen interest in the army and military matters. The Hadrian wall was built in Britain in 121 A.D. Hadrian most pressing military concerns were internal. The second and third Jewish revolts begin and ended doing his rule, and further insurrections in Britain and Mauretania occurred around 117 A.D. President Obama has shifted American economic and military interest to Asia. President Obama now face the growing military power of North Korea (Nuclear Power).

WHAT WAS HADIAN ACHIEVEMENT AT THE END OF HIS REIGN:

In 138 A.D. Hadrian died. Hadrian achievement was the end of the Roman Empire military expansion. He brought and end to the terror and persecution of Roman citizens by his predecessors. Hadrian brought more humanity toward oppressed citizens and slaves in the Empire. Hadrian was an intellectual and he introduced more art and theaters. In the East more Greek plays and more Greek classics and plays like Oedipus Rex. I Hadrian brought and improvement in the art of the Roman civilization. I believe the legacy of President Baraka Obama 1 will be of art, culture, intellectual advancement. President Obama like the Emperor Hadrian did not stop nor control the Germanic tribes from invading Roman's territories. President Obama will not prevent North Korea from obtaining more nuclear weapons, but President Obama will bring more human dignity to the oppress people of the American Empire (mitigating the harshness of the Patriot Act of 2001 which denied U.S citizen the right of Habeas Corpus).

President Obama has supported the rights and dignity for gay and homosexual people. President Obama did not support Proposition 8 in the U.S. Supreme Court in 2013. President enacted into Law the Affordable Health Care Act of 2010. The Affordable health Care Act of 2010 provided universal health care for all American citizens. President obtained an agreement with Russia and Syria to remove Syrian's chemical weapons without military conflict. President Obama further begin negotiating with Iran the cessation of their developing nuclear weapons.

President Obama had begun the open communication with the new Iran's government after thirty years of no official communication (1979-2013).

THE END OF THE BRITISH EMPIRE

The world turned upside down for the British Empire was the lost of their American colonies in the new world (1775-1783). At the close of 1774 the British Empire faced a crisis of unprecedented seriousness. The American colonies were a sought of tremendous wealth for it's London bankers and British's wealthy class. The prospect of war with Americans were greeted with dismay and disbelief inside Britain. Many agreed with the Poet Cowper, who thought that Britain and America was one country, which made a conflict unthinkable (Oliver Crowell Civil War of 1649). There was strong feeling among military men that the Americans were bluffing and that, when put to a test of arms, their cause would quickly fall apart (David Halberstam, Book Best and Brightest, 1972). The United States Army officers were discussing the U.S. involvement in the Vietnam War. The U.S. officers stated to the French that the United States military was racial superior then little Asians and the U.S. military would defeat the North Vietnamese army in six months. In 1941 Adolph Hitler speaking to his generals about the Soviet Union, that the Superior German military would defeat the Soviet union in a couple of weeks. The Russian race were inferior to the German 's race and the German race would defeat an inferior Russian race within six months (Stalingrad, disaster an entire German Army surrendered under Field Marshall, Friedrich V. Paulus, 1943). The defeat of the German's 6th army under Field Marshall Von Paulus marked the beginning of the end of the German's army war in the East on the Russia Plain (The emperor Napoleon Bonaparte was defeated in Russia in 1813 and later disaster at Waterloo 1815). The surrender of the French's army. On May 07,1954 at Dien Bien Phu under the command of General Henri Navarre, surrendered the French Army and brought an end to the French Indochina's Empire.

It took time for the reality of the situation in America to be fully understood in London. King George III and his ministers vacillated between policies of concession and coercion. By the new year King George III was convinced that Parliamentary sovereignty could only be restored by military intervention.

Foremost among the advocates of a short, sharp war was Lord George Germain, who in August replaced the more flexible Dartmouth as the Secretary of the Colonies with a mandate to mastermind operations throughout

North America (Southern General Joseph Johnson, stated that the American civil War would be a very short war 1861-65).

The policy which evolved during the early months of 1775 was therefore, both placatory and threatening. North (Prime Minister) offered conciliation with promises of fiscal concessions in return for American acknowledgment of Parliament's supremacy, and on the other hand he prepared for war. Four additional regiments of infantry were drafted to Boston, where the local commander, Lieutenant Thomas Gate, was ordered to take whatever measures he thought necessary to forestall armed resistance. A large-scale campaign was already being contemplated, and in February three major-generals, Sir William Howe, Sir Henry Clinton and John Burgoyne were appointed to command the armies which would undertake it. All were second choices since Jeffrey Amherst, who had extensive American experience and was a better general, had refused the Supreme command because of sympathies lay with the colonists.

At this point the key to the campaign was sea power. So long as supplies and reinforcement s could pass by sea between Yorktown and New York, Cornwallis and Clinton were relatively secure. This was not the case after late August when Admiral de Grasse's (French Navy, 1778 the French decided to support the American's cause against their enemy the British) fleet arrived from the west Indies and took up positions in the Chesapeake Bay. After a brief, inconclusive action the British North American squadron retired to New York, and with it went Cornwallis's chances of reinforcement or escape. As the balance of power swung against Britain, Washington, forewarned of de Grasse's intentions, broke camp and begin 450-miles dash from New York to Yorktown. The upshot was that Cornwallis, outnumbered, isolated and under bombardment, surrendered his army on 17 October. As his men marched out and laid down their arms, the band played a popular song, "The World Turned Upside Down."

For six months King George III had pig-headedly refused to acknowledge the verdict of Yorktown, and a few other diehards, including Cornwallis, who wanted to fight on. North was not one of them, in March 1782 the King accepted his resignation. The new Prime Minister Rockingham, was a moderate who opened negotiations.

THE END OF THE BRITISH DOMINATION OF INDIA:

Robert Clive had come to India, aged nineteen, in 1744 as a clerk and drifted into soldiering four years later. In England he had been an idle misfit whose despairing family (Shropshire Gentry) arranged his shipment to India. Robert Clive in about 1751 became the commander of the East Indian company private army. The East Indian Company obtained a monopoly of the trade in Indian's good and they secure the wealth of Indian by the use of their finances and their Private military. Robert Clive defeated a native army of Indians at the battle of Plassey on June 1757 and became the dominion financial power in the entire country of India. The East Indian Company remained in power in India until the Great Rebellion in 1857. In 1857 the Indians rebelled against British domination, oppression, racism, and humiliation of their culture, their women by British white men. The British put down the rebellion by massacring the Indian population. India did not gain their independence until 1947 under the leadership of Mohammad Gandhi.

WHAT WERE THE MAJOR CAUSES OF THE FALL OF BRITISH EMPIRE:

The British Empire had begun its' fall before and after the First World War. The British Could not continue to maintain security and defense of its' many colonies and oppression peoples. The Empire before the first World War had colonies in Africa, India, Asia, and some in South America. The British could no longer afford the expense of administering one quarter of the world population.

The First World War bankrupted the British Empire. Fighting the rising German Empire under the Kaiser had deleted the finances of the British and killed a l large part of the British young male population in the killing fields of Europe. The British had to borrow money from the great banks of Europe to prosecute the their war's efforts during the First World War. The British like the Roman's citizens had become physically incapable of defending the empire. The men and women moral values had falling and they sought pleasure over discipline. The British ruling class could not suppress their human desires for decadent and immoral behavior.

THE BALFOUR DECLARATION OF 1917

The Balfour Declaration was made in November 1917. The Declaration was made with the Jewish community in Britain and America and led those communities into believing that Britain world establish a Jewish State in the Middle East. On November 2, 1917 Arthur James Balfour a British the British Foreign Secretary wrote a letter to Lord Rothschild. The Rothschild was considered the most influential Jewish family in Britain. Arthur James Balfour committed Britain to establishing a Jewish state in Palestine for Jews supporting the British's War efforts in the First World War against the German Empire and her allies. Copies of the letter was dropped behind German's line by airplanes and Adolph Hitler serving as soldier in the German's Imperial Army got a copy of the letter. When Hitler became the leader of Germany he begin a campaign of placing Jews in the concentration camps. Every American president has had to address the repercussions of the letter of Arthur James Balfour's letter to Lord Rothschild on November 2,1917.

The current problems involving the Jewish State of Israel and the Palestinians in the occupied territories is a result of the Balfour Declaration of 1917. In the Balfour Declaration the British promised the Jews land in Palestine as long as the rights of the Palestinians were not violated. Since 1917 to 2013 the Jewish State of Israel has attempted to seize all of the Palestinians' lands.

The American Religious Right 's position is that God gave Israel Palestine.i would not called Arthur James Balfour God.

SYKES-PICOT AGREEMENT
OCCURRED BETWEEN NOVEMBER-MARCH OF 1916

The agreement effectively divided the Arab provinces of the Ottoman Empire outside of the Arabian peninsula into areas of future British and French control or influence. The British and French agreed to a secret treaty for dividing up the Middle East after the end of the First World War. The diplomats were Francois Georges-Picot and British Sir Mark Sykes. President Woodrow Wilson thought that Americans were fighting the Germans and their allies to make the world free for democracy. The French and the British had formulated a secret treaty for the division of the colonies after the First World War.

In 1969 I had the good fortune to meet Sir Hugh Foote the British Ambassador the United Nation while he was visiting Dr. Graham R. Hall the former United States Consul-General to India and Australia in Little Rock, Arkansas. Sir Foote had written a book called A Start In Freedom about the de-colonization of the British Empire. Sir Foote career as a British diplomat was in some of the most troubled spots around the world. But more important his book provides a fascinating record of a difficult era in world history, an era when colonies are cutting loose from dependency to become full-fledged nations in their own right, and the bitterness of nationalism has erupted throughout the world along with the idealistic call for freedom.

Sir Hugh Foote was among the last of the great Colonial Governors. Since he left the British Colonial Service, he has stepped into a new role of wider leadership in the United Nations. Sir Hugh Foote 's book gives a unique picture of the last few decades of the British Empire. Sir Foote writes in his book A Start in Freedom at the end of 1963 world tensions seem to mount and multiply. Whichever way we look we see old dangers and new failures and disappointments, in Indonesia, in Arabia, in Ghana, in Somalia, for examples. In South Africa the greater danger of a race war which must involve all Africa and the whole world.

Nelson Mandel was released from prison after the Cuban's military intervened in Angola and defeated the South African military in 1987. The United States and Israel in that battle supported the White Racist South African Government under the presidency of Ronald W. Reagan. Sir Hugh Foote gave me a history lesson of the end of the British Empire in Little Rock, Arkansas at the home of Dr. Graham R. Hall. I was twenty years old and I had just begin my journey in my love of history and an intellectual knowledge of the world outside of Little Rock, Arkansas.

FALL OF AMERICA THE LAST EUROPEAN EMPIRE:

The American Republic begin with the creation of the American Constitution in 1787 in Philadelphia. All of the original founding fathers came from the land gentry class. These were men who were about protecting their class from the commercial restrictions of the British Empire. These men who owned large agricultural estates with large slave populations. Thomas Jefferson, George Washington, James Madison were men with large estates and many black human being in servitude. The Founding Father used ancient Athena as a model in developing a democratic state. Ancient Athena was a slave state. During the time of Plato 400 B.C there were 2 million people in the city of Athens and only 40 thousand could vote. All of the remaining were slaves and poor Athenians who were landless peasants.

The United States begin as a nation with one group of people who were black being slaves were not granted the rights under the new Constitution. Ancient Rome of 509 B.C. was a republic and a slave state.

The American Republic beginning was similar to ancient Rome a small city on the Italian plains. Rome like the United States begin attacking and seizing lands of their neighbors. The new state of American conquered the native people and seized their lands. Ancient Rome attacked and conquered their neighbors' lands and seized their natural resources. The New American Republic seized the South West from Mexico through a doctrine known as Manifest Destiny.

AMERICAN CIVIL WAR ESTABLISHED THE AMERICAN EMPIRE.

The American Civil War was over the issue of slavery of Black people. Black slave's labor had been utilized to build the White House in 1790. The slaves also built the Washington Mall. The entire city of Washington was built by the labor of a slave work force. James Hoban was the city and White House Architect. Mr. Hoban contracted his slave out to work on the building of the White House project and Mr. Hoban kept the money he made on his slave's labor. Mr. Hoban's slave was his property and it was his right to keep the money made by his slave.

The beginning of the American Civil War in 1861 in South Carolina when a force of confederate soldiers fired on Fort Sumner. The Civil War was about the issue of slavery and extending slavery into new acquired territories. President Abraham Lincoln fought the entire war without seeking a congressional declaration of war. The Civil War was a police action by the President under his Powers as Commanding Chief. By President Lincoln utilizing his powers under the Constitution as Commanding chief all future Presidents Thurman and Eisenhower could prosecute the Korean War with out a declaration of war (1950-1953). President Lyndon Johnson could commit American soldiers to Vietnam without Congress declaring war. Presidents George Herbert Walker Bush in 2001 the first Gulf War and his son George W. Bush in 2003 committed American soldiers without having a declaration of war in the second Gulf War The Bush's family like the Roman's Julio-Claudia Emperors all came from the ruling class. The Bush's both father and son were of the American ruling class and they were of the white ruling class. President Baraka Obama did not come from the American white ruling class. President Obama like the Roman Emperors Trajan and Hadrian did not come from the old Roman's ruling class both came from the Roman provinces (98-117 A.D.). The Emperor Hadrian was not a military man like his predecessor Trajan. The Emperor Hadrian begin the process of consolidation of the Roman's frontiers. Hadrian ended the campaigns of military expansionism. President Obama begin the process of consolidation and restricting American military expansionism. President Obama is the first American President who is non-white and he did not come from an aristocratic family. President Obama comes from the American slave class.

HISTORICAL CHANGES IN AMERICAN DEMOGRAPHIC

President Obama won the2008 election because George W. Bush was defeated in the 2003 Second Gulf War. President Obama won his 2012 re-election because of the American demographic had changed. The United States is becoming a nation of a majority of Brown people. The new majority do not support Israel in their Middle East policy of seizing Palestinians ' lands. The American Jewish wealthy elites in the media and in Hollywood have been very racially prejudice toward American non-white populations.

The American army is historically similar to the ancient Roman's army it is made up of soldiers from the black and brown new majority. There is also a large Asians populations in the U.S. who do not feel any alliance toward the state of Israel.

AN ATTEMPT TO BRING EQUALITY TO AMERICAN
OPPRESS CITIZENS OF COLOR

Since the election of Baraka Obama (2009-2012) the racial relations in United States has deteriorated the white population feels that their position of entitlement has been negatively impacted by the election of a non-white man to the presidency.

Every society has attempted to improve the conditions of their oppressed groups. In 1872 Czar Alexander 11 attempted to bring freedom to the Russians peasants class with his Great Reform Act of 1872. The purpose of the Act was to improve the lives of peasants living on the large estates of the Russians upper class. The Russian Upper class opposed the Great Reform Act of 1872 and as result the Act failed. The failure of the Act led to the Revolution of 1905. The revolt of 1905 lead to the death of thousand of peasant by Russian troops of the Czar. Nicholas Lenin celebrated the Czar's troops killing the peasants. The Czar's troops shooting the peasant eventually led to the Russian's Revolution of 1915 and the death of the Czar Nicholas and the royal family.

The Roman attempted to bring the German tribes into the Roman Empire as citizens and under Roman's protection in 378 A.D. The Roman 's people were very racist and commercially exploited the Goth German tribes. In 378 A.D. at Adrianople the Goth defeated a Roman army under the command of Roman Emperor Valens. The entire Roman's army was destroyed by the Goth's army. The Roman's army never recovered from their defeat at Adrianople in 378 A.D.

In the Old Testament book of Genesis 45 Chapter the Prophet Joseph brought his people the Israelites into Egypt. The Egyptian Pharaoh allowed Joseph to bring his family to Egypt. The Egyptians welcome the Israelites to come into their country. The Israelites population begin to exceed the growth of the Egyptian population and the Egyptian begin to feel threatened. The United States white population are beginning to feel threatened by the growth of the Asians and Latino populations which are increasing fast then the white population (President Obama won re-election with the votes of the non-white population 2012).

In 1964 Congress passed the 1964 Civil Rights Acts granting their African-American the same Constitutional rights as the white citizens had enjoyed since the founding of the republic in 1787. The election of President Obama in 2009 has led to the increase in white racial hate groups. The Old American Confederate States of the South have all become Republican states with a majority of white people supporting all white politicians. The American Justice System is very racialist toward persons of color. The United States has the large prison population and a large part of that population are persons of color.

WHY THE AMERICAN EMPIRE HAS COME TO AN END:

We are living in the last days of the American Roman's Empire. In 2009 A.D. the American's citizen elected a new Caesar Baraka Obama 1. President Obama comes from the American's slave class (Germanic tribes in Roman Empire). President Obama succeed the last American imperialist President George W. Bush. President George W. Bush lied to the American population and led the country to a war in Iraq 2003-2012. The United States army did not win. The invincibility of the United States Army was destroyed. The German Army under Friedrich Von Paulus was defeated before the gates of Stalingrad in 1943. The German army never recovered from their defeat. The defeat at Stalingrad led to the fall of the German Empire under Adolph Hitler in 1945. The defeat of the Emperor Valens in 378 A.D. at Adrianople by the Goths led to the destruction of the Roman Empire. The Roman Army never recovered from their defeat at Adrianople in 378 A.D. by the Goths. The French Emperor Napoleon defeat of his Grand Army by in Russia in 1812 led to Napoleon final defeat at Waterloo in 1815. The French's defeat at Dien Bien Phu in 1954 by the Vietnamese General Vo Nguyen Giap brought to an end the French Indochina Empire.

CIA OVERTHREW A DEMOCRATIC ELECTED GOVERNMENT IN IRAN

In 1953 Mohammad Mossadegh was elected Prime Minister of Iran. Mossadegh came to the United States and studied Thomas Jefferson and George Washington. Mr. Mossadegh wanted to establish an American style of Republic in Iran. In 1953. The CIA and British intelligence orchestrated a coup dietat that toppled the democratically elected government of Iran. When the Iran students seized the American Embassy in 1979 the CIA coup was the reason the students seized the American Embassy in 1979. In 1951, Prime Minister Mossadegh roused Britain's ire when he nationalized the oil industry. Mossadegh argued that Iran should begin profiting from its' vast oil reserves which had been exclusively controlled by the Anglo-Iran Oil Company. The Company later became known as British Petroleum (BP). The same company was responsible for the oil leak in Louisiana Gulf in 2009. After considering military action, Britain opted for a coup d ' Etat. President Harry Thurman rejected the idea, but Dwight Eisenhower took over the White House, he ordered the CIA to embark on one of its first covert operations against a foreign government.

GEORGE W. BUSH 43TH PRESIDENT WAR IN IRAQ 2003

President George W. Bush lied to the American public about Iraq having weapon of mass destruction. The Iraq's government never had weapons of mass destruction. The Bush's Administration was planning to go to war with Iraq four years before 9-11 attack. The Bush's Administration engaged in torture of enemy combatants and just ordinary persons pick-up by the CIA. Bush's Attorney General approved the water boarding and other forms of torture of individuals (The United States first used water boarding in the Philippine in 1899-1902 against Philippine freedom fighters). George W. Bush begin the war to allegedly remove Saddam Hussein weapons of mass destruction. After thousand of death of Iraq citizens, death of 5,000 US. Soldiers and 100,000 wounded there were no weapons of mass destruction. The china secured the legal rights to the oil contracts from the Iraq's government 2007. Majority of American troops who were killed came from the U.S. lower class. They were poor white young people and the racially oppressed Latino and African-Americans. George W. Bush's nephew nor did his three daughters served in the Iraq's war. In the U.S. federal building on Temple Street in Los Angeles had pictures of all U.S. soldiers killed in the war from California in 2011. A majority of the young People killed from California were Latino soldiers.

THE COLLAPSE OF THE AMERICAN EMPIRE
AND THE REBALANCING OF THE WORLD

President Obama and his Administration are concerned about the North Korean nuclear weapons. The United States is the only country in the world that have used nuclear weapons against a nation. On August 6,1945 the U.S. dropped the nuclear bomb called Little Boy on Hiroshima killing from 40,000 to 70,000 Japanese citizens who were not military targets. The U.S. dropped the bomb at noon Japan time for the purpose of killing the most Japanese citizens who were shopping for food. The second atom bomb was dropped on Nagasaki on August 9,1945 and the U.S. killed 90,000 to 166,000 civilians and again Nagasaki was not a military target but a civilian city (During the Iraq the U.S. military alleged that they do not bomb population centers, but military targets, that was not true for Hiroshima and Nagasaki).

The North Koreans do have concerned about the U.S. will to use the nuclear bombs on Asian's cities and populations. During the Korean War General Douglas MacArthur requested the use of the Atom Bomb to use against the Chinese army in 1952. In the Vietnam War President Nixon in 1972 was contemplating using the Atom bomb against the North Vietnam military. The North Korean's Atom Bombs prevents the U.S. from using the Atom bomb.

Dean Acheson the former Secretary of State from 1949 to 1953 formulated the U.S. Foreign policy in the Korean War for the Thurman's Administration. Secretary of State Acheson appointed my mentor Dr. Graham Roots Hall to the position of Consul-General to India and Australia from 1952-1956. Dr. Hall was a graduate Yale University and Harvard Law School. Dean Acheson was also a graduate of Yale and the Harvard Law School. As young college student I lived with the Graham Halls at their home in Little Rock, Arkansas (1968-1985). During my years I lived with the Hall I met Sir Hugh Foot the British Ambassador to the United nations in 1969 and he had written a book called A Start In Freedom. I also had the good fortunate to meet John MC cook Roots the first cousin of Graham Roots Hall. John Roots was a journalist who had a close personal relationship with the Chinese Chou En-Lai who was second in command in China to Mao Tseung the founder of Modern China (1949 beginning of Chinese Republic).

WORLD EMPIRES COME AND GO

The collapse of empires is nothing new. Empires come and they go, as any student of history can Verify. In ancient times, we can read of the decadence of the Roman Empire, which brought about its collapse. In more recent times, the older among us, have witnessed the collapse of the British Empire which included one quarter of the population of the world.

Although that Empire crumbled away from 1945 on, as colony after colony became independent, in reality its real down fall had already begun in 1917. It was in that year that Great Britain went bankrupt as a result of the Great European War that started in 1914, largely by the megalomaniac Kaiser and the international armament manufacturers. Thus, in 1917 Great Britain had been forced to borrow money from financiers in order to continue the war, making political compromises to do so. From 1917 and not 1914 marked the real turning-point in world history in other ways too. It was after all in 1917 that Russian Revolution, financed from New York, took place and within a few weeks the USA had entered the European War that U.S. President Woodrow Wilson called the war to make the world safe for democracy(Wilson's Administration was very racist toward African-American Citizens in U.S.). As a result the War there began what many called the American Century, nearly a hundred years of U.S. dominance of the world, as Western Europe entered not only into its first suicide pact of 1914-1918, but also the second, from 1939-1945 (surrender of the government of Adolph Hitler, 1939-1945).

However, the collapse of the British Empire since 1945 and at more or less the same time that of other Western European Empires. Like the French, the Belgian and the Portuguese, is not the most recent collapse of Empires that we have witnessed. In some ways the collapse of the Soviet Empire, from 1989 onwards, was even more dramatic. Embroiled in a pointless, imperialistic war started in Afghanistan by a senile leader, the Soviet Empire had gone bankrupt and so lost her colonies. Like the collapsed of the British and other Western European Empires, the Soviet collapse also echoed the collapsed of the decadent American Empire, which has always provided an imperial model for imperialism.

For the bankruptcy of the Soviet Empire, like that of the British and Roman and all other Empires, were not only financial, but also spiritual and therefore moral (for spirituality is the source of morality). Almighty God allows empires because they do more good than harm. However, there always comes a decadent phase, when they begin to do more harm than good. And thus they are allowed to fall. Such was the case of the British Empire which went from noble, even Evangelical, aims and fell as a result commercial greed, in its opium wars in China, its concentration camps in South Africa and in its immoral colonial class in East Africa, India and the Caribbean. The spiritual bankruptcy of the Soviet Empire became apparent in 1976. A scholar visiting the Soviet Empire, I saw how nobody believed in Communism. I saw how country was ruled by cynicism and inertia. Already then the Communists clearly did not believe in their own ideology, but were mafia simply out to line their pockets, boredly clapping Communist gerontocrats, who themselves did not believe in their systems. Little wonder that at that time the writer Solzhenitsyn called for people there to stop living the lie. The scholar knew that once people started living for the truth, then the whole system would collapse. That is precisely the process that began after 1985. At that time the party no longer ruled, even in name, the Empire was simply ruled by a Mafia and a corrupt class.

Fortunately, since the year 2000, that criminal class has largely been eliminated and some of them now live in exile in London and Russia has revived.

However, it has become clear that this is not the last collapse of an Empire which we are to witness. For we are now witnessing the collapse of the American Empire. This is the very Empire, whose rise began ninety years ago. It seems that although the American Empire has outlasted the Soviet Empire, but less longer than any of the Western European Empires, including the Roman Empire. Although it began in 1917, its golden age was to be in the 1930s, 1940s and 1950s. Then, surely, it did more good than harm and the generosity of its people became legendary and is still warmly appreciated.

However, already in 1960s and 1970s, its power had peaked and decadence was becoming visible. Thus, it lost the Vietnam War, because, supporting a corrupt and unpopular regime, it lost the moral high ground, even against the Communist enemy. Already in the 1970s Alexander Solzhenitsyn warned the Western World of its moral bankruptcy and was disbelieved. Today, the USA, supported to some extent, or at least not actively resisted, by a spineless and venal Western Europe, has started wars against Serbia, Afghanistan and Iraq, and may even want to start a war in Iran. These are all wars which they cannot win indeed wars which it is already clearly losing. Baghdad, which means " God-given" has indeed become a graveyard for poor and unknowing American soldiers, sent to die by a government for invisible weapons of mass destruction.

Not only does the American Empire, led at best by incompetence (George W. Bush 2003-2012), at worst by greed and lies, suffer bankrupting, unwinnable and terrorizing wars which are begun out of hubris (the illusion of self-satisfied pride, and racial superiority). It also has a national debt of several trillions of dollars, which supported largely, but temporarily, by China's purchase of US government debt. Now with its illusory debt-financed boom over, the US is plunging into a crisis, as its housing bubble has burst and it faces soaring oil prices. With a ignorant down public education system, at its worst capable of turning out some of the most ill-educated and ill-behaved children in the world (not unlike the system in the UK), with a health system intent on profit and not health, with a non-existent public transport system, with a throwaway culture of unparalleled wastefulness, with an obesity crisis without precedent in human history, with a dollar so weak that American corporations are asking not to be paid in US dollars. There are those who wonder how much longer the American Empire can continue. And this is no time for Western European countries to gloat. Having passively or actively bought into the illusory American dream for so long, they too will have to help pay the cost of the real American night mare. Western Europe is dragged down by the measure of its own compromises with ideology of pride, that is imaginary superiority.

THE REBALANCING OF THE WORLD IN THE ASIATIC CENTURY

Some scholars are in despair and already preparing for the end of the world. The world did not come to an end because of the decline and fall of the British Empire. Empires come and empires go. The world did not end after the fall of the Roman Western Empire in 476A.D. The British Empire after the Second World War. A new Empire is on the rise and that new Empire is China.

The problems with moral and decadence is a common characteristics of all declining Empires. At the Battle of Issue in 332 B.C. the Greeks under the leadership of Alexander the Great fought the Persian King. The Persian King

Darius was dressed in feminine clothes made of gold. The Persian King had women make-up on. The Persians king and his nobility had become very feminine. The Romans in the last days of the Empire homosexuality existed in a majority of the Roman's men and women (Julius Caesar had sex with men and women). The Roman's army was over extended the American Army is also over extended. A Great deal of the wealth is used in paying for the military. Homosexuality is becoming a dominant lifestyle among the United States white ruling class. The US Supreme Court ruled in 2013 that Proposition 8 from California which held that marriage was only between a man and woman. The group who were support same sex marriage celebrated the US Supreme ruling that Proposition was unconstitutional and violated the rights of people who want to marriage persons of the same sex. Chief Justice John Roberts stated that his first cousin now could marriage her same sex partner.

When Augustus Caesar became Emperor the Roman Republic came to an end. The rights of their citizens under the Republic under the Dictatorship of Augustus were taken away and replaced with arbitrary rule of the Emperor.

The rights of ordinary American citizens have become reduced after the 9-11 Bombing. Congress passed the Patriot Act which reduced the rights of ordinary Americans. The American ruling class like the Roman's ruling class morals had declined. President Obama had to remove General David Petraeus from his position s as Director of the CIA for immoral conduct. President George W. Bush begun a war under false pretends and the war led to over 5,000 American soldiers being killed. There was over 40,000 American soldiers who sustained permanent injuries. There was over a million Iraq civilians killed and also sustained permanent injuries. American soldiers paid a very high price for the overthrow of Saddam Hussein as a result of the war of George W. Bush in 2003 to 2012. Captain Owen Honors was removed from his position as commander US Air craft carrier Enterprise for creating and showing an immoral sexual video with homosexual subject matter aboard ship.

The United States has made homosexuality in the US Military legal. The United States Supreme Court will rule on the legal issue of whether gay people can marry in all fifty states of the United States the summer of 2012. Homosexuality is already a normal life style among the American ruling class (former

Secretary of defense Dick Chaney 's daughter Mary is a homo sexual and living with a female partner).

The United States military sustained greatest defeat in Vietnam from 1964-1975. The US military has not recovered from their defeat after Vietnam. The US military will not be able to overcome their defeats in Iraq and Afghanistan. The German's Army was never overcame their defeat and surrender to the Russian at Stalingrad in 1943. The Roman's Army was never to overcome their defeat by the Germanic Goth tribe at Adrianople in 378 A.D. The decline and fall of any civilization is determined by the actions and behavior of their ruling class. Napoleon Bonaparte invaded Russia in 1812 with his grand army of 600,000 soldiers drawn from all over Europe. Napoleon was the Emperor of a large French Empire. Napoleon was defeated in Russia in 1812 by the Russians. Napoleon had to abandon his Army in Russia and rush back to Paris. At the battle of Waterloo 1815 Napoleon was finally defeated by a combination of European powers. Napoleon invasion of Russia led to the end of his empire at the battle of Waterloo 1815 by the British General the Duke of Wellington.

The American Empire will not collapse over night, nor will Western Europe be dragged down suddenly. This is process will take years. The United States in a period of definite decline.

The new Chinese Empire has replaced the American Empire in Asia. The Asian countries have begun looking to China as the new superpower in Asia. The American Empire military defeat in the in Afghanistan and Iraq has ended the US Empire dominance in the Middle East.

GEORGE W BUSH LAST AMERICAN IMPERIALISTIC CAESAR

May 01, 2013, is the 10 year anniversary of the famous aircraft carrier landing by George W. Bush and the Mission Accomplished " banner. Was the war with Iraq a success?

Weapons of mass destruction were never found, and to this day it was the greatest intelligence failure since Pearl Harbor. Remember how certain the administration was that Iraq possessed WMDs! Both the press and Congress went along with a carefully orchestrated propaganda campaign.

The result was that at one point some 70 percent of Americans believed that Saddam Hussein was responsible for 9/11 (The African-American population never supported the war, Congressman Barbara Lee, Berkeley, Ca. voted against the Resolution for George W. Bush to go to war, 2003). The African-American population also opposed the Vietnam War of 1965 (Gulf of Tonkin Resolution, approved President L.B. Johnson introducing US troops in Vietnam).

After the complete withdrawal from Iraq by US forces in 2011, Iraq is still bordering on civil war.

Weekly, the country witnesses sectarian violence. During 2012, 4,500 civilians deaths were attributed to this violence.

Al-Qaida is flourishing, where in 2003 they were nowhere to be found. The Al Nusra offshoot is sending fighters to Syria. The goal is to create another Islamic State.

The surge, contrary to belief, did not work. Sunni clerics are now calling for armed struggle against the Shiite majority. Protest in the Northern provinces occur every week and recently the Iraq army killed 34 protesters. Finally, there are alliances between Iran and Iraq. Iraq's closest partnership is no longer with the US, but its Shiite Neighbor Iran.

IRAQ WAS AMERICAN LOWER CLASS WAR

On 12/27/2011 I had to take a train from Oxnard, California to the United States Federal Court Building in Los Angeles, California. During my visit in the Federal Court Building there was a display dedicated to the number of young persons of California Citizenship killed in Iraq for the year of 2011. There were pictures of the young people who were killed. A majority of all the young people who were killed were Latino young people. George W. Bush stated that the Iraq was a honorable cause. George W. Bush three daughters did not served in the American army during Bush's war in Iraq. George W. Bush's nephew George W. Bush IV the son of Jeb Bush also did not served in Iraq during his uncle's war in Iraq. Vice-President Dick Chaney two daughters did not serve in the US army during the Iraq War. The United States Army like the ancient Roman Army recruited heavily among their

German conquered people or their slave class. The U.S. 's ruling class recruit also among their oppressed slave class for soldiers. The American Empire like the Roman Empire recruited among their oppressed groups for soldiers for the imperialistic army. After the Vietnam War the US Army became a professional Army not a citizen's Army. The Chinese Army where all their citizens must served their mandatory obligation of military service. The US Army is a military of poor white people and racially oppressed Black and Latino young people.

AMERICAN EMPIRE INVOLVEMENT IN SUPPRESSION
ON THE AFRICAN CONTINENT

Cuba's direct, critical and extensive role in the struggle against the apartheid regime in South Africa is little known in the West. November 5th 2005 marks the 30th anniversary of Cuba's Deployment of troops, at the request of the Angolan government, to repulse a major South African invasion of October 1975 (Same year US was defeated by the Vietnam in Saigon). In 1987-1988, a decisive battle occurred in the South-eastern Angolan town of Cuito Cuanvale 1988. When the battle occurred, it was the largest military engagement in Africa since the North African battles of the Second World War. Arrayed on one side were the armed forces of Cuba, Angola and the South West African People's Organization of (SWAPO). The Cuba's military were provided with tanks, airplanes and munitions by the Soviet Union. The other side were the South African Defense Forces, South African Territorial Forces of Pretoria – controlled Namibia. The Apartheid Regime was supported by the United States and the Government of the Jewish State of Israel. Both the United States and Israel are Apartheid States. The United States of American's buildings in Washington D.C. were built by slave labor (White House and the Washington Mall, Dr. Martin Luther King, Biography). The State of Israel maintains an apartheid conditions on the occupied Palestinians' territory and racial oppression of Arabs living in Israel (Jimmy Carter, book Apartheid State of Israel, 2006). Then President Ronald W. Reagan and Israel supported the Racial Government of South Africa. President Reagan did not have a good relationship with the US. Non-white population.

In Black Africa, particularly in Southern African the battle has attained legendary status. The Cuba's military routed the racialist apartheid army of South African supported by the United States, and Israel. The Cuban defeat of the South African military thus brought an end to white racism in the African's continent. The battle is referred to by African people as African Stalingrad and an end to US promoting racial supremacy on the African's continent. At the battle of Cuito Cuanavale, the South African Defense Forces were dealt a decisive defeat. By the Cubans defeating the South Africans military this was the first time in the 20th Century that a non-white army had dealt a severe defeat to a white military.

The defeat of South Africa by the Cuban Army brought and end to South African military threats to other African countries. President Reagan had his United nation Ambassador to arrange Ambassador arranged for Pretoria to remove their army from Angola, grant independence for Namibia, and for the releasing Nelson Mandela from prison in South Africa. The South African Defense Forces were further dealt decisive defeat on June 27, 1988 at South Western Angolan town of Tchipa a major South African offensive was soundedly routed when the South African military was encircled. President Reagan had the South African government negotiate with the Cubans, Soviets and Freedom fighters. The defeat of the South African Defense Force had similar impact as the North Vietnam defeated the United States Arm y in Vietnam in 1975. The Iraq defeated of the US army in Iraq and Afghanistan. These defeats brought to the end of the military dominance of the European Empires.

As a scholar I can see a new American life the Eastern Roman Empire which existed for a thousand years after the fall of the Western Roman Empire fell in 476 A.D. I can envision a new American under President Baraka Obama. President Obama Is a new kind of person. President Obama come from the merging of the two Americans one white and one black. President Obama re-election in 2012 was the beginning of the end of the dominance of white males in American. The demographic has changed in American. The election of 2012 demonstrated that change. The non-white population were able to re-elect a non-white man as the President of the United States. President Obama like the Roman Emperor Hadrian came from outside of the Roman's old ruling class. Hadrian was of Greek origins. The old American ruling class came from the Ivy League Universities of Yale, Harvard, George H.W. Bush, George W. Bush, and my mentor Graham R. Hall, Dean Acheson were all from the American's ruling class and graduates of Yale and Harvard Law School. President Obama has open the door for a woman President and it looks like the woman President will be Hilary R. Clinton in 2016.

The Republican Party as its currently exist will go out of existence unless the party can change their philosophy and find a leader who can identify with the changing demographic in twenty-first century American. The white population in United States is declining like the old ancient Roman population. In 2011 there are more brown babies being born in America then there are white babies. The brown population in American will change foreign policy and the direction of the American Empire in the centuries to come. The new demographic will lead to a new America which will be more justice and freedom. The new brown American will bring a new century in which the United States will be more successful economically because the new brown population can interact with a world dominated by an economic system dominated by brown people (Asians, Africans, and people from South America).

CHINA THE NEW BROWN EMPIRE OF THE TWENTY-FIRST CENTURY

China with a recorded history of 4,000 years. Chinese civilization is one of the oldest in the world. Until modern times China's development had been largely indigenous, partly because of China's isolation from other great civilizations. Chinese civilization go back as far back as 10,000 years. Chinese is the oldest continuing civilization in the history of mankind. A Chinese students today can read the same Chinese writing that has existed for over five thousand years. Chinese people do not see themselves as a nation, but as a civilization. The Chinese people and civilization have existed in the same geographical place for over 10,000 years. China has in the last thousand years has expanded their influence and power all over the Asian continent. The Chinese's Empire expanded into both Koreas and into Vietnam. Chinese Empire has expanded not so much as military conquering, but through the tributary system. The Chinese Empire saw military as the last methodology of spreading their influence.

The European nations saw military as the primary method of spreading their influence and seizing and acquiring the natural resources of their neighbors. In 2003 George W. Bush invaded Iraq for purpose of seizing their oil wealth. In 1941 Adolph Hitler invaded the Soviet Union for the purpose of seizing their oil fields for the German Empire.

Chinese scholars see history as being cyclical. The Chinese civilization has gone through the Process of greatness to decline. Civilizations like people begin life and maturate through early stages from being born to teenage to adulthood and finally to old age. The Chinese Scholars see the life of a civilization is like the life of an individual. Chinese's civilization is now in the process of being in the young adult stage and in the process of stake-off and headed toward maturity. The European Civilizations are in the process of old age and heated toward the final stages of their lives. European civilizations are in the process of dying (European civilization include the United States of America).

We live now in the Asiatic Century. China has move into the position of dominance of the military and economic sphere of the world. Russia, China, India, and Brazil are the new countries which will dictate the new world order for the foreseeable future. Chinese civilization is over seven to ten thousand year old. Some years ago I was conducting a lecturer tour in the President Ronald W. Reagan 's museum. The people who were in the tour were Chinese people. We were looking at one piece of furniture in the Reagan collection and I stated that the piece of furniture was over three hundred years old. One of the Chinese lady spoke up and stated that China have furniture that is over 5,000 years old.

China has experienced a period in their history where the country was in a period of decline.

The United States is currently experiencing an economical and military decline. The US is experiencing a racial and cultural divisions. China is a united country with its people committed to making China into a super power. Brown and Black people in United States are currently angry about their oppression by the white privilege class (white people). American white people are attempting to whole on to their entitlements which they have enjoyed since the forming of the US constitution in Philadelphia in 1787.

EMPEROR QIN SHI HUANG—FIRST EMPEROR OF CHINA

The Chinese civilization as seemed existed at the beginning of time. The historical dating of recorded history date back 5,000 years. The Chinese civilization date back almost 10,000 B.C.E. China is the oldest continuing civilization on this planet. The Chinese see their history as cyclical. The Chinese view history as a circle. Societies begin as of birth go through young adulthood and reach maturity. Once the civilization reach maturity the society begin the process of decline. American's society is in the process of decline. The Chinese's civilization is in the process of military and economical domination of the world. The Chinese are spreading their influence from Asia, Africa, to South America. The Chinese have developed economical agreement with Cuba, Brazil, Canada, Africa, and several other countries. I have spoken to my relative from Africa and they told me that the Chinese are in the process of establishing colonies through out Africa. The Chinese are also establishing colonies in South America. The Chinese world view is different then the European world' view. The Chinese believe that where Chinese people mix with the native population the people become Chinese. Anytime a person of the Chinese culture and race marriage someone of another race that child from that relationship is a Chinese person. The white European conquerors believe that they were racially superior to the non-white people and they wanted to maintain the separation of the races. In the United States it was against the law prior to 1967 for a white person and a black person to get married. The Chinese's world view is that a person of the Chinese race have sexual relations with a non Chinese the off-spring of that relationship is a Chinese person. All people in China are Chinese. All conquers of China have been eventually through sexual relations with Chinese men or women have become Chinese people. I have a friend who father is Chinese and her mother is African-American. My female friend view herself as Chinese and part of a civilization that history go back to 10,000 B.C.E. Every place the white European conquered they kept their race separated from what the European called the inferior races of black, brown and yellow people (U.S. founding fathers promoted racial superiority of white people, George Washington, Thomas Jefferson, Constitution Conference 1787). In the formulation of representation in the Congress in the American

Constitution they counted three Blacks person to make for one white person for apportionment of representation of US Congress in 1787. The European conquest of African, Asia and the America was based on the what was called the white man burden. The European included the United States philosophy was that God had selected the white man to govern all of the other races because the white man (European Civilization was superior Asian, African, and the Americas non-white cultures) civilization was superior.

QIN SHI HUANG, FIRST EMPEROR UNITED CHINA

The period of warring states was history in which several states were competing for military and economic Domination of all of China. The Chinese leader who emerged as the military and economic Power in all of China is Qin Shi Huang the First Emperor. Qin Shi Huang, born as Ying Zheng in 259 B.C. E. He was the son of the king of the Qin State. Qin Shi Huang was the Chinese equivalent to the United States George Washington (American Founding Father). At the age thirteen, he succeeded his father's legality. Ying Zheng was very aggressive and ambitious at an early age. He assumed full power at 22 by ridding himself of his premier, LuBuwel, who acted as regent while he was a minor. Like the father of Alexander The Great in 338 B.C. Phillip II defeated the combined Greek city states at Chaeronea and united all of the warring Greek states into the one state of Macedonia in 338 B.C. Ying Zheng wanted to unity and subjugate all the states like Han, Zhao, Wei, Chu, Yan and Qi by the powerful political, economic and military strength of the Qin State. Ying realized his ambition and built the first feudal and centralized empire in Chinese history in 221 B.C.E. This is what Chinese history called the Qin Dynasty (221-206 B.C.E.). Ying Zheng was the first Emperor of a united China, so he proclaimed himself Qin Shi Huang When Ying Zheng unified China, he considered his achievement by surpassing the legendary "San Huang (three emperors) and Wu Di (five sovereigns). Yeng Zheng created a new title for himself. Huangdi together with Shi (means the first), hence get the name Qin Shi Huang or Qin Shi Huangdi, which means he was the first emperor of China. He hoped his descendants would follow in his steps to rule the country for eternity.

CONTRIBUTIONS OF THE FIRST EMPEROR

Qin Shi Huang consolidated the empire by building a centralized government. Qin Shi Huang reformed politics, economy, and culture. He abolished the vassal system where people were awarded jobs because of their class and family connections. He divided the country into counties or prefectures directed ruled by the Emperor and his delegates. Qin Shi Huang reformed the tax system and introduced a law system based on the system of the Qin State. He also suppressed the scholars who opposed his government and had many of them killed.

The greatest symbol of ancient Chinese civilization is the great wall of China which was begun under the Qin Shi Huang and bears witness to Qin Shi Huang centralization of power by ordering conscription of laborers to build the Great Wall. The Great Wall was built by Qin Shi Huang to prevent marauding nomads from attacking China. Another world famous achievement is the terracotta warriors and horses in Xian, which was discovered nearby the mausoleum of the First Emperor Qin Shi Huang. Both are the wonders of Ancient China. During their construction, countless conscripts lost their lives. First Emperor wasted manpower and resources by building the wall. The Wall did not keep out the Armies of Great Khan in 1274. The United States built the White House and the Washington Mall with slave laborers 1790. The White House where President Obama and the first family resides was built by black slave laborers in 1792 (Architect James Hoban). The United States begin as a colony of Great Britain and later fought a war for independence from Great Britain in 1776 to 1781. George Washington recruited slaves as soldiers during the war of independence and he promised them freedom. The American economy was an agricultural economy based on cotton and the slave labor was essential to the cotton economy (All of the Founding Fathers who met in Philadelphia in 1787 were slave holders). The American colonists begin a war of racial holocaust against the native populations (Buried My heart at Wound Knee 1862-1982, Dee Brown). George Washington promised the African slaves that if they fought for colonists they would be granted their freedom at the end of the war. Washington had no intention of freeing the slaves. Slave's labor was valuable to an agricultural economy.

DECLINE OF THE QIN SHI HUANG THE FIRST EMPEROR

Qin Shi Huang longed for longevity, so he sent his ministers to go on quests seeking for an elixir of immortality (First Emperor was tortured at night by all of the thousand of people who he had killed so he wanted to live forever). However, death claimed him before he could find success on that matter. Qin Shi Huang departed from the world of the Living in 210 B.C.E. while traveling. Peasant uprising led by Chen Sheng and Wu Guang broke out soon after Qin Shi Huang death. The Empire of Qin Shi Huang came to an end.

QIN SHI HUANG CHINESE GEORGE WASHINGTON

Qin Shi Huang united China into an empire by conquering the warring states and building a united China. Phillip of Macedonia built the warring Greek city states into a united Greece in 338 B.C. Qin Shi Huang consolidated China by unifying the writing system which has been in existence for over five thousand years. The Chinese views of race is different then the white European Empires. The white European Empire in which United States is the primary beneficiary of is that white people are racial superior to all of brown and black people. The Chinese view is that any one who have a Chinese child with a Chinese individual become Chinese. Ancient China did not pass laws preventing people of different races and cultures from marrying Chinese people. The United States South Africa, Israel passed laws (currently exist in Israel Arab and Jews cannot marry) preventing white and non-white people from getting married. China is currently establishing colonies through Africa, South America, by marrying into the native populations. The Chinese view is that anyone marries a Chinese person that child become Chinese (Every one out of 10 person in the world is Chinese). The American empire like the former European Empire Great Britain was racially brutal to the non-white people they came in contact with (American Indians, Black slaves, Mexican people)were racially oppressed and suppressed. In the five thousand years history of China the Chinese never followed a policy of racial holocaust against people because of the color of their skin. All of the wars the United States has fought since the Second World War with Germany and her allies the United States has been killing people of non-white nations (Vietnam, Korea's war, China, Iran, Iraq, Afghanistan). During the South African War in Angola the United States and Israel supported the white racial government of South Africa. The Soviet Union and Cuba supported the native freedom fighters who were resisting white domination by the White South African Government in Pretoria (The Battle of Cuito Cuanavale 1988,the Cubans and the Defeated the South African's army supported by the US and Israel).

CENTURY OF HUMILIATION FIRST OPIUM WAR 1839-1842

The first Opium Wars was between 1839 to 1842. The cause of the war was the British was bring in opium into China from India. The British East Indian Company had a monopoly in the trade of opium from their control of India and Burma. The outbreak of the First Opium War was because the British was bring in opium into the Chinese Ports. The Chinese people were first using opium as a medical purpose for various health illnesses. The Chinese young people and middle class persons were using opium and begin the habit of smoking the drug. The British Superintendent of trade Charles Elliot with the Chinese negotiator Lin Ze-xu refused the importation of Opium in the Chinese's ports. The British East Indian company was making a great deal of money on the Chinese addiction to opium. The British Empire was built on the opium trade. The Chinese lost control over the importation of opium trade in which the British was flood the Chinese's market. Every year more Chinese were become addicted to the East Indian Company opium. The British sent in their war ships and defeated the Chinese wooden ship very easily. The British forced the Chinese in what is called the first Unequal Treaties 1839-1842. The British defeated a nation of a hundred million Chinese because of the technology advantage of the British Empire in 1842. The British forced the Chinese to sign the Treaty of Nanking August 29,1842 on board of a British War ship at the mouth of the Yangtze River. As part of the Treaty of Nanking 1842 China conceded the island of Hong Kong to Great Britain and open five treaty ports to (Canton, Amoy, Foochow, Shanghai, and Ningbo to British opium from India).The Chinese were compelled to grant trading monopoly to the British and China lost nationhood by granting the British to the British

East Indian Company the right to import and sell opium to the Chinese population. The Chinese accepted the principle of extraterritoriality that is the Western nations were not subject to Chinese's laws in the China as a country. The United States was involved in the selling and importation of opium into China. The United States was a part of the Western Powers in their forcing the Treaty of Nanking on the China people and nation in 1842. United States and the European Powers begin the process of dividing up of China as a nation and the destruction of the Chinese people by the Western powers importation of opium.

THE SECOND OPIUM WAR 1854-1860

The Second Opium War from 1854 to 1860 the Chinese attempted to restrict the amount of opium coming into china by the Western Powers, France, United States, Great Britain into Chinese ports. In May 1858, the Anglo-French naval task force captured the Taku forts near Tiensin effectively ending hostilities. France, Russia, the United States, and Great Britain then forced China to agree to open eleven ports major ports to Western trade under the terms of the Treaty of Tientsin, June of 1858. When the Chinese were slow in enacting the treaty the British shelled with their war ships forts at the mouth of the Peiho River in 1859.

The Chinese capitulated, permitting all foreigners with passports to travel freely in China, and granting Chinese who converted to Christianity full property rights. Under the terms of the convention of Peking, signed by the Chinese representative Prince Gong, brother of the Emperor Xianfeng, on October 18, 1860, the ports of Hankou, Niuzhuang, Danshui, and Nanjing were opened to foreign vessels, as were the waters of the Yangtze, and foreign missionaries were free to proselytize. China had to pay further reparations, this time ten million taels, to each of France, Great Britain, and another two million taels to British merchants for destruction of property. Finally, China conceded the port of Kowloon to Great Britain, and agreed to permit the export of indentured Chinese laborers to the Americas. Arguably, without such massive injection of cheap labor the Transcontinental railways of the United States and Canada would not have been completed so quickly and economically. On the other hand, China's humiliation led directly to the fall of the Manchu Dynasty and the social upheavals that precipitated the Boxer Rebellion of 1900. The United States Military assisted other Western Powers in putting down the Boxer Rebellion of 1900. The United States benefitted from the mass of Chinese indentured labors in building the Intercontinental Railroad in 1869.

The United States was a country built by African –Americans and Chinese slave labor. The United States, France and Great Britain fought a war with china for the purpose of opening Chinese ports up for opium and access to Chinese indenture labors to build the United States Intercontinental rail road and the British Empire. The Chinese called this period in their history the Century of Humiliation 1839-1842, First Opium War and the Second Opium War 1854 to 1860. The American Democracy was built by slave labor. The Ancient Athena Democracy of 400 B.C. was built by slave labor. The British Empire was built by the East India Company forcing the Chinese through the First and Second Opium War to open their ports to Opium.

CHAIRMAN MAO ZEDONG
THE FOUNDER OF THE MODERN CHINESE EMPIRE 1949-2013

Mao Tse-tung affectionately known by the Chinese Civilization as the Chairman Mao. Chairman Mao was born December 26,1893 he was a communist revolutionary, and the founder of the modern Chinese Empire. Chairman Mao was a Chinese nationalist first and a communist last. Mao was the founding father of the People's Republic of China from its establishment in 1949.

Born the son of a wealthy farmer in Shaoshan, Hunan, Mao adopted a Chinese Nationalist and anti-imperialist outlook in early life. Mao like Chinese of his generation had observed how China had been conquered and divided up by the Western Powers.

In 1839 through 1842 Great Britain invaded China and forced China to accept the opening of their ports to British opium from India. The Chinese population became addicted to opium from India. The British Empire made a great deal of money from their opium trade. The United States was also one of the Western Powers that were involved in forcing the Chinese to accept opium in their ports for the population to consumption. As a result of the Opium War of 1839 to 1842 the British obtained the colony of Hong Kong for a hundred years lease (Hong Kong was returned in 2000 A.D). The First Opium War ended with the Chinese being forced to sign the Treaty of Nanking August 29, 1842.

The Second Opium War started because the Chinese officials attempted to stop the British, the United States, France from bring Opium into their ports and destroying their people health and lives for profit. The Chinese was forced by the by the Western Powers Great Britain, United States, France to accept the conditions under the terms of the Convention of Peking, signed by Prince Gong, brother of the Chinese Emperor Xianfeng on October 18,1860. The Convention forced the Chinese to open five more of their ports to the Western Powers bring opium into China for the consumption of the Chinese people. China ceded the port of Kowloon to Great Britain, and agreed to permit the export of indentured Chinese laborers to the Americas. Arguably, without such a massive injection of cheap laborers the United States could not have built the Intercontinental Railways. The Western Powers degraded the Chinese leaders, people, culture and the Chinese women by giving the Chinese women sexual diseases. After the Communist came to power in 1949 the Communist eliminated all sexual diseases. Chinese Historians called this period in their history the Century of Humiliation.

In 1922 Chairman Mao and the Chinese Communist party agreed to an alliance with the Kuomintang, a national revolutionary party led by Chiang Kai-Shek. Chairman Mao formed a peasant army and he fought the Japanese who invaded China in 1937. General Chiang Kai-Shek was supported by the United States and Chairman Mao was supported by the Communist in Russia. Chaing Kai-Shek and Chairman Mao agreed to an alliance to fight the Japanese. The Alliance came to an end after the Japanese surrendered in 1945. Chairman Mao and General Chiang Kai-Shek fought a war for the control of China. In 1949 Chair Mao and his Communist Party of China won the war and forced General Chiang Kai-Shek to flee to the Island of Taiwan.

From 1949 to 2012 China has become a world super power militarily and economically. China has replaced the United States as the new world super power. The United States after losing the wars in Iraq and Afghanistan has become a second rate military and economical Power.

Chairman Mao historical achievements in China is compared to the historical achievements of the three American Presidents. President Abraham Lincoln defeated the Southern secessionists and preserved the union. Chair Mao defeated the Nationalist under General Chiang Kai –Shek. Chairman Mao expanded the Chinese's economy and changed the lives of millions of Chinese citizens. President Lyndon Bain Johnson passed the 1964 Civil Rights Acts which brought the African- American population their constitution rights. Chair Mao introduced changes in the Chinese economy by his land reform policies. Chairman Mao passed laws protecting women and granting women the same rights as men. Chairman Mao extended educational opportunities to all Chinese people. Chairman Mao provided universal health benefits to all Chinese people. Chair Mao modernized the Chinese People Army.

CHIANG KAI-SHEK (1887-1975)

Chiang Kai- Shek was a Chinese nationalist who led the Chinese National Party in opposition to Chairman Mao Chinese Communist Party. Chiang Kai-Shek was born October 31,1887 in Zhejiang, an eastern coastal province of China. His father was a merchant. At age 18 years old Chiang Kai-Shek received military training college in Japan. He returned to China to take part in the uprising that overthrew the Qing Dynasty and established a Chinese Republic. Dr. Sun Yat-Sen and earlier Chinese National who was the president of the first Chinese Republic in 1911. After the death of Dr. Sun in 1928 Chiang became the leader of the Chinese National Party. Chiang spearheaded the successful campaign to unite all of China under the National Government based at Nanjing. In 1928 Chiang led a military campaign that suppressed the Chinese Communist party under Chairman Mao.

In 1937, the Japanese launched a full –scale invasion of China. In 1941 the Japanese bombed The United States Naval base at Pearl harbor and the US declared War on Japan. Chiang formed and alliance with U.S. against Japan. In 1946, civil war broke out between the Chiang Chinese national Party and the Communist Party under the leadership of Chairman Mao. Chairman

Mao and the Communist were victorious And Chairman Mao established the People's Republic of China. During the civil war between General Chiang Kai-Shek and Chairman Mao the United States supported General Chiang Kai-Shek. General Chiang and the remaining National Party fled to the to the Island of Taiwan. The US continues to their day military support of the Chinese nationalists on the small island of Taiwan. After the death of General Chiang Kai-Shek the United Nations granted to the People's Republic of China the seat in the Security Council of the United Nations. In 1964 The People's Republic of China became a nuclear power by detonating the first Chinese's nuclear bomb.

The Second Chinese Empire established by Chairman Mao is the dominant military and economic power in Asia. The First Chinese Emperor Qin Shi Huang established the first Chinese Empire in 221 B.C. Chairman Mao two thousand years later established the Second Chinese Empire in 1949. In 2013 The Chinese Empire dominates all of Asia. The US. Still have military bases in Asia, although the US is in total decline after being defeated in by the Vietnam Communists in 1975.

HO CHI MINH / VIETNAM DR. MARTIN LUTHER KING

Ho Chi Minh was born in Vietnam in 1890. His father, Nguyen Sinh Huy was a teacher employed by the French. Ho's father had a reputation for being extremely intelligent but his unwillingness to learn the French language resulted in his loss of his job. The White South Africans forced their Black population to learn their language (Biography of Nelson Mandela). Ho's father to survive, Nguyen Snh Huy was forced to travel throughout Vietnam, offering his services to the peasants. This help usually involved writing letters and providing medical care. As a nationalist, Nguyen taught his children to resist the rule of the French. Not surprisingly, they all grew up to be committed nationalists willing to fight for Vietnamese independence.

Ho's sister obtained employment working for the French Army. She used this position to steal weapons that she hoped one day would be used to drive the French out of Vietnam. She was eventually caught and was sentenced to life imprisonment. Although, Ho's father had taught his children to resist

French domination. Nguyen Sinh Huy decided to send Ho to a French School. This the father felt would prepare the son to resist French domination.

Ho finally settled in Paris in 1917. Here he read books by Karl Marx and other Left-wing writers he became converted d to communism. In December,1920 the French Communistic Party was formed. Ho became one of its founder members. Ho, like the rest of the French Communist Party, had been inspired by the Russian Revolution. In 1924, he visited the Soviet Union. While in Moscow, Ho wrote to a friend that it was the duty of all communists to return to their own country to : to make contact with the masses to awaken, organize, unite and train them, and lead them to fight for freedom and independence.

Ho Chi Minh attended the Paris Peace Conference in 1919 at the end of the First World War. The United States President Woodrow Wilson had drawn up his plan for the war peace after the war. President Wilson was recommending all of the European Powers' colonies be allowed to have freedom and self determination. Ho while working in Paris decided to obtain an audience with President Wilson to request freedom for the Vietnamese people. President Wilson refused to meet with Ho Chi Minh. President Wilson's plan for freedom and self determination for people did not include brown Vietnamese people under French oppression. During President Wilson 's Administration racial discrimination in the US had become very harsh and oppressive for African-Americans (1919 racial riots in St. Louise). After the surrender of the Japanese the French refused to recognize the Democratic Republic of Vietnam that had been declared by Ho Chi Minh and soon fight broke out between the French and the forces of Ho Chi Minh.

When it became clear that France was becoming involved in a long-drawn our war the French public grew tired of the war 1946-1952. The United States public also grew tired of the Vietnam war and demanded an end to the war (President Johnson introduced US troops into Vietnam, 1965, Gulf of Tonkin Resolution). The French military needed a quick victory as a result French General Navarre's drew up a plan to defeat the Vietminh forces at Dien Bien Phu. The French's army was surrounded by the Vietnamese under the command of General Vo Nguyen Giap the Asian Napoleon in 1954 at Diem Bien Phu. The French surrendered on May 7,1954. French casualties totaled over 7,000 and further 11,000 soldiers were taken prisoner.

ASIAN NAPOLEON VO NGUYEN GIAP
BORN AUGUST 25,1911

Vo Nguyen Giap was born 25 August 1911 in Quang Binh province French Indochina. Giap's father and mother worked on a farm. Giap's father was a minor government official and a committed nationalist. Giap's father Vo Quang and mother Nguyen Thi Kien played a part in uprising against the French in 1885 and 1888. Giap's father was arrested by the French and died in prison. Giap's two sisters and brother were also arrested by the French for anti-government activities. Giap's brother and one of his sisters died as a result of French's imprisonment. Giap had lost his entire family before he was ten years old. Giap was a general in the Vietnam People's Army and a politician. Giap was a commander in two wars: the first Indochina War (1946-1954) and the Vietnam War (1960-1975). He directed the following historically significant battles : Dien Bien Phu (1954), the Tet Offensive (1968), the Easter Offensive (1972), and the final Ho Chi Minh Campaign (1975). Giap is considered as one of the greatest military generals of modern military history. Giap defeated the French army in 1954 and the American military war machine in 1968 (Tet Offensive) and the Ho Chi Minh Campaign of 1975.

In 1939, Giap married fellow socialist Nguyen Thi Quang Thai. Their marriage was brief as he was forced to flee to China later that following the French outlawing of Communism. While in exile, his wife's father, sister, and sister-in-law were arrested and executed by the French. In China, Giap joined with Ho Chi Minh, the founder of the Vietnam Independence League (Vietminh). Between 1944 and 1945, Giap returned to Vietnam to organize guerilla activity against the Japanese and later to fight and defeat the French at Dien Bien Phu in 1954. General Giap also defeated the US. Army in Vietnam during the Tet Offense of 1968. The Tet Offensive convinced the American Public that the Vietnam War could not be won on the battle field.

The Vietnam War ended the perceived invincibility of the US Army. The defeat of the United States In Vietnam marked the end of the military campaigns of European armies on the Asiatic Continent. General Douglas MacArthur in 1953 stated that a European army could not win a war on the Asiatic Continent. General MacArthur also requested the use of the Atom Bomb

Cou[

ANDREW JACKSON:
President Jackson begin the genocide against
Native Americans 1836 Trial of Tears and
seizure of Cherokee for their lands.

President James Polk provoked a war with
with Mexico 1846-1848 to seize California,
Texas, Arizona, Colorado, Manifest Destiny.

President Abraham Lincoln the Civil War
by using his powers under the Constitution
as Commanding chief (1861-1865) Civil War
Congress did not declare War.

Theodore Roosevelt

President Theodore Roosevelt begin
U.S. imperialist expansion over sea
during the Spanish-American War 1898.

Courtesy of Franklin D. Roosevelt

President Franklin D. Roosevelt conducted
the Second World War and begin the U.S.
World dominance as a world Empire.

Courtesy of Leo Stern

President Harry Thurman 1945-1950
expansion of the U.S. Empire in Asia
as a result of Korean War . The
Korean War was a non-declared war.

President Lyndon B. Johnson 1963-1968.
Johnson further expanded the U.S. Empire
in Asia with Vietnam War (beginning of
the decline of U.S. Empire)

Ronald Reagan

President Ronald W. Reagan 1980-1988.
Reagan begun the expansion of the U.S.
Empire after Vietnam War.

Reagan Receives Landslide

Carter Makes an Early Conce

Clinton Holds Lead In Re-election Bid; Bryant Winning

Governor Bill Clinton, facing one of the strongest Republican gubernatorial challenges in the state's history from Frank D. White, a Little Rock businessman, was leading, but only barely, in initial returns Tuesday night.

With 161 of 2,811 precincts reporting, the vote was:

Clinton 26,408
White 25,094

Judge,

GOP Poll In Ea

From UPI, AP and
Republican Ro
ceived a landslide
ceded defeat at 8:50
nationwide television
gan, was ready to co
With 32,466, or
cincts counted in the

Courtesy of The George !

President George Herbert Walker Bush
1988-1991. President Bush begin the
U.S. empire expansion in the Middle East
with first Iraq War 1990.

Courtesy of Clinton Presidential Materia

I worked in Bill Clinton's 1983 campaign
for Governor in Little Rock, Arkansas

FRANK WHITE
DEFEATED
BILL CLINTON
FOR GOVERNOR
OF ARKANSAS
1980.

GOVER
WHITE
TO YOU
GOD BLESS
MARY
WHITE

— Staff Photo by Hank Wilson

'Contented' Challenger, Wife with Supporter

Frank D. White, the Republican gubernatorial nominee, and his wife Gay (left) greet a supporter, Mrs. Sue Woolsey, after voting at the First Christian Church on Mississippi Avenue. The Whites were accompanied by White's daughter Elizabeth, 18, a college freshman, who voted for the first time. A campaign worker described White's mood on election day as "excitedly contented."

(Continued From Page 1A.)

Passage of Amendment 59 Indicated by Early Returns

Two years of legislative debate, a petition drive that received 190,000 voter signatures and a media campaign conservatively estimated to have cost $750,000 preceded Tuesday's vote on proposed Amendment 59.

It was assumed, almost from the beginning, that the campaign would succeed, if only on the attractiveness of the ballot title that promised "tax relief." Mid-October polls showed that 70 per cent of voters approved of it.

Proponents of 59 warned that taxes statewide would rise by an average of 174 per cent and could increase by up to 700 per cent if the measure was not adopted. However, they campaigned knowing that their effort, even if successful, could be nullified by the court-ordered property tax reappraisal.

The charter's property-tax provision would supersede that of 59, which was to amend the existing Constitution.

Urged Support for Both

Many backers of Amendment 59, including some members of the Statewide Committee for Amendment 59, urged voters to vote for both 59 and the new constitution and thus take two shots at dealing with increased property taxes brought on by the 1979 court-ordered property tax reappraisal.

Other 59 backers, such as the Arkansas Farm Bureau Federation, invested campaign resources solely in the campaign for 59, whose provisions the Farm Bureau felt were preferable to those of the constitution. The 59 campaign theme urged Arkansans to "get tough on taxes" by voting for the amendment. Its symbol was a pugnacious-looking bulldog.

The only groups to challenge Amendment 59 seriously were Arkansas Community Organizations for Reform Now, which campaigned on a shoestring budget;

Proposal for Legislature

early lead. With 161 precincts out of 2,811 had polled 52 per cent to 44 per cent for Mr

It was a far cry from the 65 per cent Mr. Carter garnered in the state in 1976 when he unseated President Gerald R. Ford.

Lyndell Lay of North Little Rock, chairman of the Carter-Mondale Campaign in Arkansas, said early in the evening that he hoped the president would hold the state. It was the only hope among the small group of sad faced faithful who showed up at the campaign headquarters at Little Rock as early returns indicated a national landslide for Reagan before the Arkansas polls even closed.

The campaign of National Unity candidate John Anderson and Patrick Lucey slipped to 3 per cent of the state's vote in the early returns. Other independent or minor parties were showing little or no strength. The Libertarian Party headed by Ed Clark showed 1 per cent.

The Citizens Group Party of Barry Commoner had only 74 votes, representing less than 1 per cent, and two parties — the People Before Profits organization headed by Gus Hall and the National Statesman's Party of Benjamin C. Bubar — had no votes at all.

The totals for the seven tickets were:

Carter	24,328
Reagan	29,251
Anderson	1,778
Clark	482
Commoner	103
Buber	0
Hall	0

Except for very brief trips to Texarkana, which played host to Mr. Carter and Reagan in an eight-day period, no major candidates came to Arkansas after they were nominated.

Reagan's wife Nancy and Bush's son Jeb visited the state in the late stages of the campaign. The Reagan campaign also had

(Continued

Early I

Show

Being

kansas AFL
sas Educati
the conserv
new docume
It had the
county gove
the financia
was seeking
limits, and
minded or
League of
Common Ca

Much of
constitutio
issues. The
sued a repo
governmen
a year. Co
delegates
of dollars
tax exemp
nishings ai
a drop in
homeowne
assessmen

Other
Committee
stitution
Fight In
Higher Ta
sions that
lature and
raise mor
Committe
the legisl
ings and t
sors to v
land on

Continued From Page 1A.)

Clinton Barely Leads In Governor's Race; Bryant Also Winning

rienced and incapable administrator and a man who had never met a payroll, saying repeatedly that he would run the state like a business. The governor said he had done just that and cited the new purchasing law, more efficient money management methods and the hiring of successful businessmen to head four state departments.

White, who became known during the campaign for fiery old-fashioned stump speeches that lambasted Mr. Clinton, said late in the race that he would win because the issues were "car tags and Cubans." Indeed, he did attempt through his campaign advertising to make those the issues.

He said Mr. Clinton showed insensitivity to the economic plight of Arkansans by backing and signing legislation that raised car license and title transfer fees dramatically. He said he would roll back the increases, but he hedged late in the campaign when asked specifically how he would do it. He suggested a flat $25 license fee for all cars, but that actually would raise the fees on about 250,000 vehicles. He also said he might use the state's general fund to pay for highways, which Mr. Clinton said had never been done and would be bad policy because it would take money from education and necessitate a tax increase.

The governor defended his highway package as necessary to the continuation of a road program in the state, citing the deterioration caused by severe winter weather three years in a row, the fact that no new sources of income had been developed for highways in several years and that the federal government was trimming its highway funds for the state. Legislators, county judges and mayors began defending the governor late in the campaign.

'Contented' Ch

Frank D. White, the Republican gubernnee, and his wife Gay (left) greet Mrs. Sue Woolsey, after voting at th tian Church on Mississippi Avenue.

(Continued From Page 1A.)

Passage
Indicated

Courtesy of www.georgebush.com

President George W. Bush (junior) 2000-
2008. Junior begin the Second Iraq .
Junior was the last imperialist Caesar.
Junior administration marked the
historical transition from a European
Civilization dominance of the world
to a Chinese economical and military
Empire dominance of the world.

President Barack Obama 2008-2016
President Obama has begun the campaign
to reduce the U.S. Empire (Emperor
Hadrian 117-128 A.D. Adrian Wall
stop the expansion of the Roman Empire).

against China's military forces that had cross over into Korea in 1953. President Thurman denied his request. President Nixon considered using a nuclear bomb against the North Vietnam military in 1972 in the Vietnam War.

President Obama is currently dealing with the issue of a nuclear armed North Korea. President Obama negotiators are asking the North Koreans to eliminate their nuclear weapons. The US. is the only country in the world that have used nuclear bombs against an adversary by bombing of two large Japanese cities during World War Two. Will the US give up its nuclear weapons? The United States does not have a technological advantage over its adversaries and the U.S. cannot match the Chinese nor North Korea in their size of their military forces. The Unites States has not asked the Israel to give up their nuclear weapons. Western powers conquered the armies of non-white countries by their technological advantages of over non-white countries. The army of Saddam Hussein Iraq would not have been invaded by the US if he had the nuclear bomb. The North Koreans will not be attacked by US as a result of having nuclear weapons. The Iranian will never be attacked by Us nor Israel if they develop nuclear weapons. The United States arm forces after Vietnam is a mercenary army. During the Vietnam War the US military used the draft to fill their military ranks. The draft proved to be unfair to non-white young people. A majority of the combat units in Vietnam were made up of African-Americans and Latino-Americans young people. White Americans like former President George W. Bush used his father connections to avoid the draft by enrolling in the Texas National Guard. Therefore, George W. Bush was able to avoid combat service in the Vietnam War. Vice-President Dick Chaney used his marriage and support of his children as a reason to avoid military services in Vietnam. President candidate Mitt Romney used his father's connections to avoid military service during the Vietnam War. During the Iraq War of 2003 President Bush stated that the War was an honorable cause. President Bush's two daughters nor his nephew George W. Bush IV the son of Jeb Bush never served during the Iraq War of 2003-2012. The Iraq War of 2003 was fought by the sons and daughters of the poor. The Roman Army of the First Century A.D. were made up of a large force of Germans mercenaries not Roman's citizens. The Republican Party is made of white men calling for war in the Middle East are made up of white men who have not served in the US 's military. Mitt Romney's five sons have never served in the US. Military. The US. Military is comprised of sons and daughters of the non-white populations who are the racially oppressed in US. Sons and daughters of the racially oppressed are being asked to carry the burden of the American Empire. During the American Civil War rich men could pay poor people to serve in the Civil War in their place. Young Theodore Roosevelt's father James hired a poor person to fight in the Civil War in his place. The Chinese and North Korean armies are people 's armies where the Chinese and North Korean citizens are drafted to fight in their armies. The Chinese and North Korean armies are not made up of the racially oppressed. The United States cannot reinstitute the draft. The white privileged classes will not serve in the military and risk being killed or permanently injuries. After the Napoleonic Wars the French mothers demanded that their sons not fight to defend the Empire. In 1870 the French established the French Foreign Legion for the purpose of defending the French Empire (Dien Bien Phu, 1954 General Navarre commanded a force of French Legionaries).

CONCLUSION: AMERICAN THE LAST EUROPEAN WHITE EMPIRE

President Barack Obama inherited an American Empire in decline. The United States begin as an Empire at the beginning of the First World War. The British the American cousins' Empire came to an end at the end of the First World War. The United States inherited the White Man Burden that the British had relinquished as a result of their debt that Britain had developed as a result of fighting in the Great War.

In 1953, the CIA and British intelligence orchestrated a coup d'Etat that toppled the democratically elected government of Iran. The government of Mohammad Mossadegh. In 1951, Prime Minister Mossadegh roused the British's anger when he nationalized the oil industry. Mossadegh argued that Iran should begin profiting from its vast oil reserves which had been exclusively controlled by the Anglo-Iranian Oil Company. The company later became known as British as British Petroleum (BP).

After considering military action, Britain opted for a coup d'Etat. President Harry Thurman rejected the idea, but when Dwight Eisenhower took over the White House, he ordered the CIA to embark on one of its first covert operations against a foreign government. The coup was led by an agent named Kermit Roosevelt, the grandson of President Theodore Roosevelt. The CIA leaned on a young insecure Shah to issue a decree dismissing Mossadegh as Primer Minister. Kermit Roosevelt had help from Norman Schwarzkopf (father of General Norman Schwarzkopf). It was because of the United States part in deposing Mossadegh in 1953 the Young Iranian Guard seized the American Embassy in 1979. The Iranian people are still angry about the United States part in overthrowing Mohammad Mossadegh in 1953 Coup by British Intelligence with aid and support of the CIA. The Iranians are in the process of developing a nuclear bomb. The British supported a coup d'Etat for the purpose of retaining control of the Iran's natural resource of oil.

DID GOD OR BRITISH FOREIGN SECRETARY JAMES ARTHUR BALFOUR ASSIGNED THE JEWS TO PALESTINE?

The Balfour Declaration was made in November 1917. The Balfour Declaration committed Great Britain to establishing a Jewish State in the Middle East. Arthur James Balfour British Foreign Secretary wrote a letter to Lord Rothschild and in that letter Balfour committed Britain to allowing the Jews to establish a State in Palestine. The Jews reward for supporting the British's war efforts during the First World War was the state of Israel (Palestine).

All Jews in the countries that were allies of German during the First World War had to do whatever they could to ensure that Germany lost the war. The Jews that were German's citizens had to do whatever they could in German to sabotage the German's efforts war. The Arthur James Balfour's letter to Lord Rothschild was accepted by the Jewish community in German as marching orders to do whatever they could to destroy Germany's war efforts. The German Jewish community worked to ensure that Great Britain won the First World War. The British also promised the Arabs their independence for their support of the British's war efforts against Imperial Germany.

President Obama inherited difficult problems between the Arabs and the Jewish State of Israel. God did not give the land of Palestine to the European Jews its was Arthur James Balfour in his letter to Lord Rothschild in 1917.

President Obama find himself committed to defending Israel because of a letter written to Lord Rothschild in 1917 by Arthur James Balfour a diplomat in the British Foreign Office during the First World War. The people of the Middle East are angry because of the British betrayal. The British also promised their Middle Eastern allies during the First World War that they would be granted independence and Palestine and Jerusalem would be returned after the First World War. The British had no intentions of returning Palestine and Jerusalem to their Arabs' allies after the war. The British remained in Iran after the war to exploit and seize the Iranian's oil.

SYKES-PICOT AGREEMENT

The French Diplomat Francois Georges-Picot and the British Sir Mark Sykes and the Russian Tsarist Government also signed an agreement which divided up the lands and people of the Middle East. The French and British negotiated with the Russian representative an agreement which allocated the control of Sea and River Jordan, Jordan, Southern Iraq, and parts of Haifa to Acre. This secret agreement occurred between Britain and France between November of 1915 and March of 1916. The British and the French had formulated an agreement on dividing up the former colonies of the Ottoman Empire who had an alliance with Imperial German during the First World War. The French and Britain had agreed to divide up the colonies of German and the Ottoman Turks before the end of the First World War. The British had betrayed the Arabs their allies during the First World War. The British had agreed with the Arabs for their support of the British's war efforts that they would obtain independence. The British had no intentions of granting independence to their Arab allies. President Obama is attempting to resolve a problem between the Arabs and the State of Israel that is related to the British and French betrayal of the Arabs during the First World War. The United States and the European Powers have supported Israel against the Arab's aspirations for freedom and their state of Palestine.

CUBAN PEOPLE FIGHT FOR FREEDOM AGAINST US IMPERIALISM

The United States obtained control over Cuba during the Spanish American War of 1898. After the war Cuba had become vacation spot for American tourists who were looking for prostitution, drugs, and gambling. Gangers like Meyer Lansky had made Cuba into a territory of sin, immorality, and hedonism for the American leisure population. The Unites States companies controlled and owned 40 percent of the Cuban sugar industries, all of the cattle ranches, 90 percent of the mineral wealth, 80 percent of the utilities, and all of the oil industries. The Cuban population extremely poor. The US had imported their racial apartheid system from main land U.S. to the island of Cuba. The Cuban people who were of dark color suffered extreme racial discrimination as a result of American White people living and coming to the Island.

The US supported the Cuban dictator Fulgencio Baptista who was very brutal to the Cuban population. Baptista murdered thousands of Cuban people, he brought drugs to the island with the mafia, prostitution, gambling, crime boss Meyer Lansky. In 1959 the young Fidel Castro with his freedom fighters defeated the forces of Baptista and the US imperialism. Castro brought universal health care to all Cubans, he end racial discrimination based on skin color, he ended prostitution, drugs importation, and gambling, and the US companies ownership of Cuban land and resources with Cuban Revolution of 1959.

The United States in 2013 still maintains sanction against the Cuban people. The CIA had made many attempts on the life of Fidel Castro. The Cuban's health system is the best health providing system in the Americas including the United States.

Fidel Castro has opposed the United States imperialism throughout the Third World. In 1988 a Cuban expeditionary army fought the Racist Apartheid Army of South African in Angola in a little village called Cuito Cuanavale and the Cuban Army of Fidel Castro destroyed the white apartheid army of South Africa. The white apartheid army of South Africa was supported by the United States and the nation of Israel. The African countries called the Battle South Africa Stalingrad (Adolph Hitler 6th Army surrendered to the Soviet's Georgy Zhukov, 1943). The Germany army defeat at Stalingrad in 1943 end the image of invincibility of the German Army and later led to the Surrender of Germany in 1945. The defeat of the South African Defense Force by the Cuban's Army led to the freedom of Nelson Mandela out of the South African's prison. President Reagan and his Chief of Staff Dick Chaney opposed the South Africans granting freedom to Nelson Mandela in 1988 after the Cuban great victory over the South African Army at Cuito Cuavanale. The Cuban's Army defeat of the South Africans army proved that an army of people of color could defeat a white army (Vietnamese defeated the United States Army in 1975). (Stalin's General The Life of Georgy Zhukov, Roberts, Geoffrey, 2012), (The Tragedy of Vietnam, Causes and Consequences, Hearden, Patrick, J., 2006).

President Obama inherited a foreign policy which historically goes back to military and diplomatic policies made during and after the First World War. The people in the Middle East will have to solve their own problems President Obama is not a miracle worker. President Obama inherited an American Army that have been defeated in Iraq and Afghanistan. The American army is experiencing problems with sexual exploitation by soldiers of the lower and higher ranks. Military personnel are allowed to engage in homosexual relationships. A homosexual military personnel do not have to conceal his or her homosexuality. The Summer of 2013 the U.S supreme court will ruled that people of the same sex can marry in the United States (US Supreme Court ruled that same sex can marry in June of 2013).

SEPTEMBER 11,1973 CIA COUP IN CHILE

It was on September 11, 1973 that the democratically-elected government of Salvador Allende was overthrown in a CIA-backed military coup. President Richard Nixon and his National Security Advisor Henry Kissinger encouraged and supported Augusto Pinochet to seize power in Chile and murder Salvador Allend Chile new President. Augusto Pinochet went on to kill thousands of Chileans, jailed, tortured and driven thousand into exile. In 1953 President Dwight Eisenhower and ordered the CIA to embark on its first covert operations against a foreign government. Richard M. Nixon President Eisenhower's Vice-President twenty years later ordered the CIA to overthrow a democratically-elected president. President Eisenhower ordered the CIA to overthrown Mohammad Mossadegh Iran democratically-elected president.

Salvador Allende of Chile and Mohammad Mossadegh of Iran before both men were elected they visited American and studied both George Washington and Thomas Jefferson. Allende of Chile and Mossadegh of Iran utilized the ideas of Washington and Jefferson in forming their governments. The United States overthrown both presidents for the mineral wealth of their countries. The United States in two hundred years had developed from a small republic into a world empire which like their British cousins were murdering and killing people all over the world for their natural resources (Stephen Kinzer author of all the Shah's Men : An American coup and The Roots of Middle East Terror and Baruch College Professor Ervand Abrahamian).

SADDAM HUSSEIN HERO OF GEORGE HERBERT WALKER BUSH 41
AND PRESIDENT GEORGE W. BUSH 43 PRESIDENT

Saddam Hussein the President of Iraq was the hand pick president of Iraq by both President George Herbert Walker Bush and his son George W. Bush. Saddam Hussein journey to power in Iraq was encouraged and supported by the Bush's connections and their establishment. Both father and son had selected Saddam Hussein like President Nixon selection of Augusto Pinochet in Chile in 1973 coup and President Eisenhower selection of the Young Shah in the Iranian coup of 1953.

PRESIDENT BARACK OBAMA INHERITED
THE UNITED STATES IMPERIALIST HISTORY

The United States imperialist history begin with the early colonies holocaust against the Native American people from 1607 to 1892. Dee Alexander Brown great book Bury My Heart At Wounded Knee tell the sad story of the United States genocide against Native American people. The United States democracy was built by slave labor like the ancient democracy of Athens of Plato 400 B.C. The White House and Washington Mall was built by slave labor by James Hoban the American Architect. James Hoban designed and built the White House by using African-American slave labors in 1790-1792. The United States also engaged in holocaust against native American peoples (Bury My heart At Wounded Knee, Dee Brown, 1970). The United States has a history of racism against Asian people who were brought to U.S. to build the Intercontinental Rail road 1869. In 1882 the U.S. Congress passed the Chinese Exclusion Act. The purpose of the Chinese Exclusion Act was to prevent Asian people from coming and settling in the United States. The U.S. allowed the Chinese male laborers to come to the U.S to work. The U.S. government would not allow the Chinese male laborers to bring their wives and girl friends. The U.S. government did not want the Chinese laborers to remain in the U.S. The white apartheid power establishment believed that the Chinese race was inferior to pure white Anglo Saxon culture and race (Virginia Vs. Loving, 1967, U.S. Supreme Court held that white people and non-white People could get married).

PRESIDENT OBAMA FINANCIAL AND MILITARY SUPPORT OF STATE OF ISRAEL

Arthur James Balfour British Foreign Secretary wrote a letter to Lord Rothschild the wealthy Jewish British citizen. In his letter Balfour committed Britain to supporting the establishment of a European Jewish state in Palestine if the Jews would support the British's efforts War efforts against the Imperial German Empire in first World War.

The British had also promised the Arabs that they could obtain their independence for their support of the British's War efforts against Germany during the First World War. The German people discovered the Balfour's letter to Lord Rothschild and Adolph Hitler begin his campaign of holocaust against European Jews.

ASIATIC JEWS INVOLVEMENT IN AMERICAN SLAVE TRADE

During the American Civil War Jews fought for the Old Confederacy. Judah P. Benjamin was Secretary of War for the Confederate States of America. Simon Baruch was the Quartermaster for the Confederate States of America during the American Civil War from 1861-to 1865. David de Leon was the Surgeon General of the Confederate States of America during the Civil War 1861 to 1865. European Jews established and support the African slave trade and Jewish scholars were proud of the money that Jewish traders made in the African Slave trade for over three hundred years (Carnegie Institute of Technology, Pittsburgh, Penn., Elizabeth Donnan, 4 vol. Documents illustrative of the history of the slave trade to America, Washington D.C. 1930-1935). The Jews created and established and made money on the African slave trade and the holocaust against African people. I would add that the Africans were also engaged in the capture and trading of slaves.

THE FIRST OPIUM WAR 1839 TO 1842
AND SECOND OPIUM WAR 1858 TO 1860

The British Empire was built on opium from India and Afghanistan by the British East India Company. The British fought a war with China called the First Opium War 1839 to 1842. The British forced the Chinese to open their ports to British's opium from India. The Chinese's government was concerned about the millions of Chinese people becoming addictive to British's opium. The British through the Treaty of Nanking 1842 forced the Chinese to open their ports to British's opium and the British obtained the colony of Hong Kong. The United States also benefitted from the opium trade. The United States was also involved in the selling of opium to the Chinese people.

The Second Opium War from 1858 to 1860 was fought over the right that the European powers desire to have more Chinese's ports opened to the selling of opium to the Chinese people. The Chinese called this period in their history the Century of Humiliation. The European Powers won the Second Opium War and forced the Chinese to open all of their ports to opium. The United States was one of the European Powers that military was involved in defeating the Chinese's Army. The European Powers defeated the Chinese through their technological superiority over the inferior Chinese Army. In the 21th Century China has the technological advantage over the White European Powers including the United States. The Treaty of 1860 that ended the Second Opium War provided that the United States would obtained indentured Chinese laborers to build the United States Intercontinental Railroad of 1869.

The United States benefitted from the Second Opium War by securing Chinese slave labors to build the Intercontinental Rail road in America. The

U.S. benefitted from the treaty by allowing American Business interest to sell opium in more Chinese's ports to poor Chinese people. The American Empire was also built on opium like their British cousin's Empire.

PRESIDENT OBAMA'S GOALS FOR THE 21ST CENTURY

President Obama like the Roman Emperor Hadrian is an academic and his approach is to apply intellectual thought to problems. President Obama must encourage the European Jews in Israel to settle their economic and military problems with the Palestinian people. The United States cannot solve their problems. President Obama must work with the new Chinese Empire to address the new economic and military challenges in the Korean Peninsula involving North Korea nuclear power.

The New Europe with Germany being clearly the New European economic super power must be encouraged to undertake the economic and military burden presently carried by the United States. The U.S. must begin to closed down U.S. military bases throughout the world to save money. The US 's wealthy class must pay their fair share of taxes. The US 's military must returned to the citizen draft for military service for all of our citizens rich and poor. The German tribes that were brought in to the Roman Empire's territory were a very moral and religious people. The Latino population is also a very religious and moral people who will bring more richness and pride in hard work. The African-American people brought music, art, jazz, rock-in-roll and our dominance in sports throughout the world (Tennis Serene Williams, and golf Tiger woods). The Asians population will bring science, mathematics achievements and history and tradition, Muslin population will bring religion and devotion to families values, science, literature, and history.

All Americans must prepare for the new frontier of culture changes and embrace this new frontier. All of these new people will make America the new bright city on a hill. America again will be the leader in the new frontiers and the new challenges of the 21th Century.

What role can the United States play in the 21th Century? The U.S. like all world empires we are in the period in our history when the empire is declining economically and militarily. We will have to accommodate ourselves to the new reality. The American white males do not rule the world any more. The U.S. is becoming a brown country. President Obama won the 2012 election by carrying a majority of the votes of non-white voters. The Republican party is a majority party of white people. The Republican Party is made up of white people who cannot accept the new reality of becoming a minority and no longer seen by brown people as racially superior.

The 2012 Census reported that last year 2011 that whites had fallen to a minority among newborns. The brown populations were out producing the white population. Fueled by immigration and high birth rates, particularly among Hispanics, racial and ethnic minorities were growing more rapidly in number s than the white population. The decline in the U.S. white population has been occurring more quickly than expected, resulting in the first natural decrease for whites, deaths of whites exceeding their births. William H. Frey, a demographer at the Brooking Institute stated that there are more white people dying then there are white babies being born. Los Angeles, California is a city where the non-white population out numbers the white population. In 2043 the American white population will be a minority in a majority of all of the States in the United States.

The non-white population will inherit all of the historical injustices that the American empire perpetrated against the entire world of a majority of brown people. The Chinese are doing very well in their foreign policies with the developing countries like Brazil, Iraq, South America, Africa, and Asia, Singapore, Indonesia, Vietnam, and South East Asia. The Chinese do not have a history of racism, exploitation, militarism, and CIA assassinations, and torture of foreign citizens (Water boarding in Iraq, Philippine War of 1899-1902).

The United States has a four hundred year history of racism against their own brown populations, African-American slavery, holocaust against native populations, racial injustice against Hispanic populations, and the Asian populations.

The China is currently expanding their empire all over the world. In ancient China the Chinese did not expand beyond their borders. The time China did it was for defense against invaders from the Asiatic Plains. The Chinese Empire is currently expanding in Africa, South America, an Asia. The Chinese are currently building a large canal in Nicaragua for the Nicaragua Government. This new canal will rival American Panama Canal built by Theodore

Roosevelt. President Roosevelt assisted the rebels in Panama who wanted independence from Colombia (1903). The rebels declared independence from Colombia and the President Roosevelt supported the rebels. President Roosevelt assisted the insurgents because he wanted to build the canal not because he supported any people democracy. President Roosevelt was an imperialist. What the Americans achieve with their military the Chinese have achieved with money. The U.S. invaded Iraq to seize the Iraq's oil fields in 2003. The Chinese were granted the oil contracts by the Iraq's Government. The Chinese never fired a shot and obtained access to the Iraq's Government oil contracts.

CAN THE UNITED STATES REMAIN A UNITED COUNTRY?

The larger challenge for the United States is to remain a united country when the white population become a minority. The non-white president must be a person who can unite all of the different races and cultures that he or she will inherit. The United States will be a country where race will be an issue that will divide the country. The United States will no longer be an empire. The U.S. will be a country among other industrialized countries of the world. The U.S. will be a country similar to Canada. There will be universal medical care for all of their citizens like Canada and France. The U.S. will have a smaller military and a military which the country can afford. A majority of the soldiers will be soldiers of color. The U.S. military is currently recruiting children of color as officers in the U.S. military. All young people of college age will be guaranteed a free college education. The U.S. will again take the lead in environmental technologies and global peace and security. The United States will become like the Soviet Empire after their decline. The Soviet Empire begin to break up and the separate countries wanted their independence. Will the non-white majority of American people of color want their own country. Chinese Americans do not want to be assimilated into the greater American white culture. Latino-Americans and African-Americans do not want to be assimilated into the American white culture. None of the none-white people have any historical connection with the American white founding fathers of the Constitution of 1787. All of the American Founding fathers were slave holders and owners. The new majority will be people of color who have no historical connections with the American founding fathers who were all white men and property owners (slaves were property). The 1787 U.S. Constitution made slavery legal in Article IV, Section 1, Provision 3, " If your property run away to a free state (New York) a Virginia slave owner had the legal right to go to New York and secure his property and return his property to Virginia (George Washington, Thomas Jefferson, James Madison, and Andrew Jackson were all slave owners, Dred Scott Decision, 1857, Roger B. Taney, Chief Justice Supreme Court).

Former President William Jefferson Clinton was being interviewed by inter- national news media and he stated that Los Angeles was a majority city of people of color. Former President Clinton further stated that the nation with so many different cultural and race groups do not have any symbolism to hold the country together. The United States is facing a similar problem that the old Soviet Union confronted in the late 1980s. The Old Soviet Empire imploded with all of the small states seeking and obtaining their independence from the Soviet Empire. The United States is headed toward the same division that embroiled the old Soviet Empire.

I wanted to explore the recent trial of the man accused of killing the young seventeen years old African-American young Trayvon Martin in Florida. A jury of six women founded Mr. George Zimmerman not guilty of profiling and killing the young man. African-American males and Latino males are racially profiled every day in the United States. The United States history begin with the racial profiling people of color when the white European settled in the new world. The new settlers begin immediately killing the non-white people. The United States initiated a campaign of racial genocide against native people with the purpose of total extermination of all native people (Dee Brown, 1972 Buried My heart At Wounded Knee). All of the American's founding fathers were slaveholders. Both Thomas Jefferson and George Washington were slaveholder. The American White House where President Obama and his family currently resides was built by slave laborers. The United States is the only nation among the developed nations where their capitols were build by slave laborers.

The United States attempted to provide their slave laborers freedom during the Great Civil Right Struggle of the 1960s. The Trayvon Martin 's trial has indicated that the Civil Right's laws have not made the former slaves equal under the law.

Since the Second World War the United States as a world empire has been on a campaign to suppress non-white people all over the world. In 2003 George W. Bush's war in Iraq killed over 500,000 Iraq civilians. In 2004 an American solders went into a village in Iraq called Haditha and massacred over 24 civilians (old women, children and old men). The justification for the killings were that a American convoy was attacked by an improvised explosive device that killed an American Marine (My Lai Vietnam 1968). Five American soldiers in Afghanistan went on a killing campaign of killing young and unarmed Afghanistan citizens and cutting fingers, and other parts of the corpses for trophies (Sgt. Calvin Gibbs). In 2012 another American soldier in Afghanistan went on trial for killing sixteen women, children and old men in a small village in Afghanistan. All of the civilians were unarmed women, old men and small children. The United States perpetrate a genocide against non-white people within the US and non-white people over sea. American white soldiers carries their racial hate of people of color throughout the American Empire (Christopher Bales,2012).

Equal justice for non-white people in the United States will come when the people of color begin to assume positions where they can have input within the decision making policies of the American establishment (The modern State of South Africa, under Nelson Mandela, 2013). The American Empire is in the process of declining and the white population are afraid for their future in a non-white people controlled America.

I have taken interested scholars through the journey and horrors of empire. All of the Empires of the world history whether the Egyptian, Babylonian, Persian, Greek, Roman, the Spanish, British and the American Empire utilized terror, suppression, and genocide against any group or individuals that threatened their power and existence of the empire.

Within every empire God (Muslin God, Buddhism, Christianity) creates a humanitarian individual (Abraham Lincoln, Mahatma Gandhi, Dr. Martin Luther King, Hugh Thompson). I would like to share a little history about an American Hero who is not known to the larger world. I would like share the history of Hugh Thompson. Who was Hugh Thompson? Hugh Clowers

Thompson,jr. was born on April 15,1943, in Atlanta, Georgia. He grew up in rural Stone Mountain, Georgia, raised by his strict parents. After dropping out of Troy state University, he volunteered for the United States Navy in 1961 and served with a Seabee construction unit from 1961 to 1968. Hugh Thompson is best known for his role in stopping the My Lai Massacre, in which a group of US Army soldiers tortured and killed several hundred unarmed Vietnamese civilians, mutilating their bodies after they had been murdered. Mr. Thompson said that he approached the apparently peaceful My Lai hamlet from the air in his scout helicopter and he did not realize what was going on until he saw a US captain nudge a wounded Vietnamese girl with his boot, then kill her. According to the Army, the three men landed the helicopter in the line of fire between American ground troops and fleeting Vietnamese civilians to prevent their murder by U.S. Troops. Helicopter pilot Hugh Thompson, door gunner Lawrence Colburn and Crew chief Glenn Andreotta landed their helicopter between American Troops rampaging through My Lai village and the local people. There were 500 innocent people, including many women, children and elderly, were killed by the Americans, who were angry at the deaths of their comrades. The My Lai Massacre led to the court martial of platoon leader Lieutenant William Calley. Calley was sentenced to life in jail, but released three years later by then President Richard M. Nixon. Hugh Thompson intervened in the killing by placing his helicopter between the US troops who were killing the Vietnamese civilians and he threatened to open fire on the US. Troops if they did not cease killing the Vietnamese civilians. In 1969 Hugh Thompson was summoned to Washington D.C. and appeared before a special closed hearing of the House Armed Services Committee. Hugh Thompson was criticized by South Carolina Democrat Mendel Rivers who demanded that Hugh Thompson be court martial for pointing a weapon at US troops and threatening to fire. Hugh Thompson received death threats, and mutilated animals were left on his front door steps. The military establishment first attempted to deny that My Lai had occurred. Hugh Thompson retired from the army with a rank of major.

Almost 30 years to the day after the My Lai Massacre on March 16,1968, Hugh Thompson, Glenn Andreotta, and Lawrence Colburn were decorated for their heroism at My Lai. Glenn Andreotta had died in combat three weeks after the My Lai Massacre, and so was honored posthumously for his bravery in intervening in Lieutenant William Calley's troop killing Vietnamese civilians at My Lai march 16,1968.

Hugh Thompson died at the age of 62 after an extensive treatment for cancer. Hugh Thompson died on January 6,2006 at the Veteran Affairs Medical Center in Pineville, Louisiana. Lawrence Colburn his life long friend was at his bed side. Hugh Thompson, Lawrence Colburn and Glenn Andreotta are saintly men representing the best in American 's Civilization. These outstanding men make me proud to call myself an American.

Russian's academic Igor Panarin has been predicting the U.S. will fall apart in 2010. Panarin admits, that few people took his argument seriously. Dr. Panarin stated in his academic theory that the U.S. will fall because of economic, and moral collapse (legalizing of homosexuality) will trigger a civil war and eventual breakup of the U.S. Professor Panarin, a 50 years old, is not a fringe figure. Dr. Panarin is a former KGB Analyst, and the Dean of the Russian Foreign Ministry's Academy for future diplomats. Dr. Panarin stated in his belief that mass immigration, economic decline (U.S. economy is declining 2% per year and China's economy is increasing 10% per year), moral degradation will trigger a civil war and the decline of the dollar (Canadian's dollars are stronger than U.S. dollars). Dr.Panarin is receiving wide acceptance by the Russian intellectual class. Dr. Panarin's ideas are now being widely discussed among local experts. Dr. Panarin presented his theory at a recent roundtable discussion at the Russian Foreign Ministry. Russian top international relations school has hosted him as the keynote speaker. During an appearance on the state TV channel Rossiya, the station cut between his comments and TV footage of lines at soup kitchens and crowds of homeless people in the U.S.

Dr. Panarin stated that he based his forecast on classified data supplied to him by KGB Analysts who study historical trends in the U.S. Professor Panarin predicts that economic, financial and demographic trends (white people becoming a minority by 2020) will provoke political and social crisis in the U.S. Dr. Panarin stated that wealthier states in US will with hold funds from the federal government and effectively secede from the union (Governor Perry of Texas during the 2012 made a statement concerning withdrawing from the federal government). Dr. Panarin stated in his theory that social unrest and civil war will result from the economic and moral decline of the U.S. The U.S. will split along ethnic lines (continuation of the racial divide), and foreign powers will move in and divide up of the U.S (China declined in the 17th century and the European powers divided up the country),(After Alexander the Great death in 323 B.C the Greek city-states divided into separate political states warring among themselves). The U.S. for 400 years has had a racial problem which persist today in the 21th century. The U.S. racial problem is reaching a point wherefore the problem can only be resolved through the division of the country among it's different cultural and racial groups. This scholar believes that the U.S. will not become divided like the Greek city states. The U.S. is on a long historical journey in which there will be equality for all of their suppressed and disenfranchised people of color. This scholar believes that the U.S. will produce people of good will who will prevail and lead America to a new revolution of human dignity and freedom.

LEGACY OF BARACK OBAMA
THE 44TH PRESIDENT OF UNITED STATES OF AMERICA

President Obama was successful in removing the American' military from Iraq and Afghanistan. President Obama being a scholarly individual gives a great deal of thought before he considers any action (military). Wherefore, President George W. Bush was not a scholar nor a great thinker. President Bush rushed into the Iraq War without giving the military campaign any realistic thought. President Bush made the similar mistake Adolph Hitler made in June, of 1941 with his invasion of the Soviet Union. President Bush like Hitler thought that his (U.S. white people) race was superior to the Iraq people. Napoleon made a similar miscalculation when he invaded the Russian Empire under Czar Alexander the First in 1812. The army of Hitler was destroyed at Stalingrad in 1943. The army of Napoleon suffered similar defeat in Russia in 1812.

President George W. Bush requested from the U.S. congress and House a joint resolution giving him absolute power to commit U.S military forces to Iraq as a result of 9/11. Both Congress and the House voted to give the President Bush to approval to commit American Military to an invasion of Iraq. In 1933 Adolph Hitler claimed that the Communists had Planted a bomb a bomb in the German's parliament and he requested emergency dictate powers and the German's parliament passed the Enabling Act giving Hitler absolute dictate powers. President George W. Bush stated in his book Decision Points that he personally approved torturing of the Iraq and Afghanistan prisoners under CIA supervision. Bush's justice department gave the President the legal justification for his campaign of torturing prisoners under CIA control (Decision Points, Crown Publishers, 2010). The U.S. military had a long history of using water boarding Prisoners. The U.S. Military used water boarding against the Filipino insurgents during the during the Filipino War of 1899-1902.

PRESIDENT BARACK OBAMA NEW UNIVERSAL HEALTH CARE LAW/ AFFORDABLE HEALTH CARE ACT 2010.

President Obama was able to accomplish universal health care for all Americans. President Obama will be remembered by historians as the first American president to enact universal health care for all Americans. President Obama was the first President to obtain a significant treaty with the Russians in the Middle East without firing a shot. The Russians agreed to encourage and oversee Bashar Assad of Syria removal of Syria's chemical weapons and placing the chemical weapons under United nation's supervision.

President 's efforts at getting the universal health care act enacted has confirmed his place in American History as one of our greatest Presidents. President Obama stated that Abraham Lincoln was his role model as a great president. President Obama with his obtaining the universal health care for all Americans and the treaty with the Russians for the removal of the chemical weapons of Bashar Al-Assad has confirmed his place in American History as a great president as was his role model Abraham Lincoln.

President Obama's Administration has achieved another major breakthrough the new Iranian leader and his foreign policy diplomat has met with President Obama's Secretary of State John Kerry and begin state to state conversation about major foreign Policy issues. The United States and Iran has not had a serious diplomatic exchange since 1979 when Jimmy Carter met with the former Shah of Iran. President Obama will probably be ranked among American Historians as one of our greatest Presidents of the twentieth century.

President Obama has Secretary of State has met with Iranian representatives to discuss the Iranian nuclear weapon program.

African-Americans as a racial group came to America as slaves. They have made extraordinary contributions to the American Civilization. There have never been group of people in world history who have overcome such extreme oppression and made such out standing contributions to a society that one enslaved their people. Douglas A. Blackmon a Southern Historian in his book Slavery By Another Name recorded the historical struggles of African- Americans after the Civil War to obtain freedom and dignity for their families and children.

President Obama as a Democratic President has ensured that Hillary Clinton will be the first female president of the United States in January of 2017. This scholar pray to God that he will be alive to celebrate that historic day. African-Americans in the 2016 Presidential Election will be Hillary Clinton key to her success in many elections in the Southern States. Hilary Clinton receive a majority of the votes from the African-American's communities. Hilary Clinton will be able to hold together the non-white population voters that she will inherited from Barack Obama. In the 2016 Presidential election Hilary Clinton was not able to obtain a high turn out of black voters and she lost the election Donald Trump. Donald Trump became the 45th fifth U.S. President on January 20, 2017. Trump took a page out of Adolph Hitler's play book when Hitler became the Chancellor of Germany in 1933. Hitler became Chancellor of Germany in 1933 through a back room deal. Trump became President in 2017 as a result of the Electorial College established by Alexander Hamilton in 1787 for the purpose of preventing poor people from selecting the U.S. President. Hitler promised the German's people that he would make Germany great again. Hitler led Germany to disaster in World War II. Trump will lead U.S to destruction and the final decline of U.S. Empire. Trump election will lead to complete moral decline of U.S. Hitler surrounded himself with followers who were morally depraved and racists. Trump will select people who are just as morally depraved as himself.

President Obama inherited the legacy of foreign policies of past American's Presidents. The United States since the founding of the country has followed a historical Campaign of hate and destruction of people and countries of color since the end of the Second World War (Korean War 1950-1953,

Vietnam War 1965-1975, The First Iraq War 2000-2001 to the Second Iraq War 2003-14). The State of Israel was created by the British Empire with the Balfour Declaration in 1915-1917. The British promised that they would give the Jews Palestine if they support the British's war efforts against the Imperialist Germany Empire (1914-1918 First World War). The British also promised the Arabs that they would obtain independence For their countries. The British had no intentions of allowing the Arabs to have Independence. The British Empire needed the Oil of the Arabs' countries (Iran over throw of the Iranian 's President in 1953 with the assist of the CIA).

President Obama inherited the historical oppression, exploitation, and genocide by the American Empire against Black and Brown people and their countries.

The United States supports the State of Israel in the their military campaign of genocide against the People of Palestine with funding and military equipment. The U.S. claimed to be an impartial arbitrator at the same time providing the State of Israel with gun, bombs, and airplanes to kill the Palestinian people (Jewish people were the primary financial beneficiaries of African-American slavery). The Jewish Financial community financially benefited from African-American Slave trade and genocide (Jews and African-American Slavery, 1800-1865).

THE PRESIDENCY OF WILLIAM JEFFERSON CLINTON

William Jefferson Clinton was born on August 19, 1946 in Arkansas. Clinton was Both a student leader and a skill musician. He was an alumnus of Georgetown University where he was Phi Beta Kappa and Kappa Psi and he earned a Rhodes Scholarship to attend the University of Oxford. Clinton married Hillary Rodham Clinton who served as President Obama' Secretary of State (Senator from New York) from 2009 to 2013. Hillary was Senator from New York from 2001 to 2009. Both of the Clintons received Law degrees from Yale law School.

Bill Clinton was Governor of the State of Arkansas from January 11,1983 to December 12,1992. I worked in Bill Clinton's campaign for Governor in 1983. Clinton ran against Frank White a Republican Governor. Frank White was a graduate of the Service Academy and a banker in Little Rock, Arkansas before he sought the office of Governor. I knew Mr. white through his former wife Mary Hollenberg. Mary 's father was the childhood friend of my mentor, employer and friend Graham Roots Hall. Dr. Henry Hollenberg was an outstanding medical physician in Little Rock, Arkansas. Dr. Hollenberg was and outstanding human being as well as being an excellent medical doctor.

Clinton was elected president in 1992, defeating incumbent George H.W. Bush. Clinton presided over the longest period of peacetime economic expansion in American history. Clinton became the first Democrat since Franklin Delano Roosevelt to be elected president twice. Clinton passed welfare reform and State Children's Health Insurance program, providing health coverage for millions of children. In 1998, Clinton was impeached for perjury before a grand jury and obstruction of justice during a lawsuit against him, both related to the scandal involving a White House intern. Clinton was acquitted by the Senate and served his complete term in office. The congressional Budget Office reported a budget surplus between the years 1998 and 2000, the last three years of Clinton's Administration.

During the years Clinton was Governor of Arkansas Hillary worked as a lawyer at the Rose Law Firm in Little Rock, Arkansas and G. Gaston Williams was her boss at the Rose Law Firm. Mr. G. Gaston Williams contacted me in California after I had returned from a visit with of Elizabeth Lewis's brother Bill Tyler in New York. Bill Tyler was a good and kind man I was his house guest in New York for a short visit to the big city in 1987. The reason Mr. Gaston contacted me was my dear friend Louise Boaz Hall had passed-way (wife of Graham Roots Hall, former United States Consul-General to India and Australia, 1952-1956).

Bill Clinton was a great democratic president he created a budgetary surplus for the country and he made me proud to be an Arkansan.

African-Americans have made great contributions to American Civilization. Tiger Woods integrated America golf and was a role models for children of color who Thought that they could never play the sport. Venus and Serene Williams integrated U.S. Tennis and introduced a sport to all children of color.

Jesse Owens made history by winning four gold medals in the 1936 Olympics. Despite the politically charged atmosphere of the Berlin Games, Jesse

Owens was adored by the German public. Germans sought his autograph, and Jesse Owens was cheered by the stadium crowd.

Though Jesse Owens was an African-American (therefore despised by the Nazis as non-Aryan), he could move about Berlin freely, stay in the same hotels as whites, use public facilities without hindrance. By contrast, Jesse Owens face segregation, restriction of movement, and other indignities at his home in the United States. The irony of this was not lost on Jesse Owens. When the American press reported that Hitler had deliberately avoided acknowledging Jesse Owens's victories and refusing to shake Jesse Owens's hand, Jesse Owens said that was not true. Jesse Owens stated that when he passed the Chancellor, Jesse Owens said that Hitler arose, waved his hand at Jesses Owens and Jesse Owens stated that he waved back at the German's leader. Jesses Owens stated that when he returned to the United States after a ticker-tape parade on Fifth Avenue, Jesse Owens stated that he had to take the freight elevator at the Waldorf-Astoria to a room where he was the honored guest. " Jesse Owens stated that Hitler did not snub me", Owens said. "It was our president (FDR) who snubbed me stated Owens." The president did not even send Owens a telegram (Bobrick, Benson, A Passion For Victory, The story of the Olympics in Ancient and Early Modern Times, Alfred A. Knopf, 2012).

PRESIDENT OBAMA'S OBSERVATION
OF THE HISTORY OF RACISM IN U.S. HISTORY

The President gave his observation of the Fergusson Grand jury decision to not Indict the white police officer for killing an unarmed 18 years old black male. There is a historical injustice in the U.S. Criminal Justice System toward individuals of color in the U.S. In 1992, smoke rose above the skyline of Los Angeles where businesses and abandoned cars burned following the acquittal of white police officers in the beating of Rodney King. In 2013 thousand s protested across the nation when George Zimmerman was acquitted in the shooting death of seventeen years old teenager Trayvon Martin by and all white all female jury (one person of color) in Florida. In Furman V. George 1972 the U.S. Supreme Court ruled by a 5-4 that capital punishment was unconstitutional. The death penalty qualified as cruel and unusual punishment because executions were arbitrary and capricious ways, especially in regard to race (majority of Black and Brown males were being to executed).

There have been four unarmed black men killed by white police officers in which a majority all white grand Juries declined to indict white police officers for the killing of men of color (State of Israel courts always never indict security forces for killing unarmed Palestinians). Black people was brought as slaves into the Virginia colony in 1619 and there have been a white racist campaign by the legal systems to brutalize, torture, perpetrate genocide on people of African heritage (all persons of color, Native Americans, Bury My Heart At Wounded Knee, 1970, De Brown).

There was Eric Garner a black male was killed by white police officers in New York and a majority all white Grand Jury declined to indict a white police officer for the killing. John Crawford a black male was killed while shopping at a Walt Mart in Beaver Creek, Ohio. Mr. Crawford was holding and handling a toy BB gun. The Police was called to the Walt Mart and they came in shooting and killed Mr. Crawford. There was a white male carrying a side arm and he was not stopped nor killed by the same police officers who had just killed Mr. Crawford. The white police officers who killed Mr. Crawford while he was holding a toy BB gun were not indicted for killing Mr. Crawford. Mr. Ezell Ford an African-American was alleged to have tackled the lead police officer and went for the officer's weapon reported by a Los Angeles police officer. A local news report interviewed a witness who identified as herself as Mr. Ford's mother and she stated that Mr. Ford was shot by the police officer while he was lying on the ground. The Los Angeles District Attorney is investigating the case. Mr. Dante Parker of Victorville, California resident was stopped by the Victorville police officers while riding his bicycle. Mr. parker did not have a criminal record. A scuffle ensued between the police officers and the 36 years old African-American male and the police officer tasered Mr. Park repeatedly when he resisted an arrest. Mr. parker begin breathing heavily and he was taken to the hospital according to witnesses. Mr. Parker died at the hospital as a result of the repeatedly tasered by the police officers. Mr. Parker had not committed any crime nor was he wanted for committing a crime. In 2013 Mr. Alfonso Limon a 21 years old Latino male was shot several time by the Oxnard, California police officers while they were chasing two others Latino males for an alleged traffic stop violations. The Oxnard Police officers alleged that the two suspects had fired shots at the officers. Mr. Limon was shoot seven times because he was a Latino male jogging in area where the police was chasing the two Latino suspects. The Ventura County District Attorney Greg Totten investigated the shooting of Mr. Limon by the Oxnard Police Officers and concluded that the shooting of Mr. Limon seven time while he Was jogging was an accident. Mr. Greg Totten has a history of not filing charges against Police officers that killed persons of color.

Mr. Michael Hanline walked out of prison after spending 36 years in prison for allegedly killing And individual in Ventura county. The Chief Prosecutor who prosecuted Mr. Hanline deliberately Concealed information that would have proven that Mr. Hanline was innocent. The California Innocence Project a program out of California Western School of law worked on Mr. Hanline's case for 15 years before they were able to clear him of the allege murder. Mr. Totten's colleague Mr. Robert McCullough in Ferguson, Missouri declined to prosecute the Ferguson white police officer that shot and killed the unarmed black teenager Michael Brown. I served on the 1996-1997 Ventura County Grand Jury. The Fore person told the jurors that the then Ventura county District Attorney Mr. Michael Bradbury had informed the Fore person that he would not bring a case to the Grand Jury unless he was assured of an indictment. The Fore person interviewed the Grand Jurors individually and told the jurors what the DA had said. The Fore person stated that the District Attorney was going to submit a case for a criminal indictment. The Fore person stated that he would like all of the jurors to vote to indict the individual. A female on the Grand Jury told the Fore person that Deshay Ford had to be convinced to vote to indict the individual. The Fore person asked to speak to me in private and he ask me to vote to indict the individual. I told the Fore person that I would support his position. We indicted the individual before the Grand Jury received the case and the evidence.

President Obama stated that racism is American as the Fourth of July and to ignore that fact does not make it go away. President Obama made this remark to Black Entertainment Television during an interview. The largely African-American audience already knew this be to a fact from their history in the United States. The First Lady Michele Obama had a white female assigned to her dormitory at Princeton in 1985. The white female Catherine Donnelly from New Orleans upon learning that Michele Robinson was an African-American female refused to share her dormitory room with a Black female student Michele (Obama)Robinson. The first Lady stated that the white students at Princeton would not socialize with the African-American students.

In 1787 the Founding Fathers that met in Philadelphia to write and approve the Constitution of 1787 were all slaveholders. George Washington and Thomas Jefferson who both were later to become presidents of the new republic were both slave owners.

The new Constitution of 1787 in Article IV, Section 1.3, "stated that no person held to service or labor in one state under the laws therefore, escaping into another, shall, in consequence of any law or regulation therein, be discharged from such service or labor, but shall be delivered upon claim of party to whom such service or labor may be due." If a slave which was property ran away to a free state the owner from the slave state had the legal right under the 1787 Constitution under Article IV, Section 1.3 to demand that his slave be returned to him or her. Under Article I, Section 2.1, established the House of Representatives, stated that members were to be selected by the people and chosen every two years. Some of the Southern states had more slaves then free white men (only white men owning property could vote). The Founding father agree to allow three slaves as one white man (Three Fifths of all other persons). In the 1787 Constitution established in Article 1, Section 2.1 that the Southern States could count three slaves for one white man for Representation in the U.S. House of Representatives.

The parents of Michael Brown the unarmed teenager that was killed in Ferguson, Missouri by a white police officer appeared before the United nations Committee on Human Rights to ask for justice for their son. A United nations panel criticized the U.S. Criminal Justice System for their handling of the killing of an unarmed Black teenager. The United Nations further criticized the U.S. for their handling of detainees at Guantanamo Bay, in Cuba. The United Nations criticized the U.S. for their practices of how police perpetrated torture, and brutality toward Black and Brown persons. The United nations further stated that U.S. Criminal Justice System, racial profiling violated persons of color human rights.

Senator Dianne Feinstein released a report about the Central Intelligence Agency crimes of torturing, water boarding (U.S. in 1898-1902 water boarded Philippine insurgents In their war for independence). The CIA interrogators did not torture for information, but for the joy of inflicting pain on their detainees (Russian's Historian and Noble Prize winner in 1970, Aleksandr Solzhenitsyn, Gulag Archipelago, the KGB interrogators tortured not for information, but for the joy of torturing prisoners). President George W. bush, Vice-President Dick Cheney, Attorney-General Alberto Gonzales, and Assistant John Yoo gave legal approval to the CIA for their torturing and brutality. Secretary of State Colin Powell opposed the CIA torturing and brutality toward detainees.

The Russian Scholar Igor Panarin at the Russian Diplomatic Academy stated that the U.S. would implode as the Soviet Empire in the 1980s because of racial divisions and cultural conflicts. The Black and Brown people do not believe that they can obtain Justice in the American Criminal Justice System. Black people have been in North American for four hundred years and still are subjected to racial profiling, police brutality and injustice in the American Democracy. People of color do not believe that they will ever obtain justice in the American Criminal Justice System.

The American Empire is threatened internally and externally by their brutality and torturing of their own black and brown populations and it's brutality and torturing abroad (Middle Eastern persons). The American Empire is experiencing similar problems of decline as the Ancient Roman Empire.

SENATOR DIANNE FEINSTEIN'S REPORT OF CIA TORTURING
AND BRUTALITY OF DETAINEES AROUND WORLD

President George W. Bush invasion of Iraq was for the purpose of seizing the Iraq's oil Reserves in 2003. Bush's goals for the invasion was the same reason Adolph Hitler invaded the Soviet Union on June, 1941. Hitler wanted to seize the Russian's oil fields for his German's Empire. Hitler invaded without legal provocation. The Soviet Union was not contemplating invading Hitler's Germany. Bush experienced the similar defeat in 2003 as Hitler had experienced at Stalingrad in 1943.

Senator Feinstein in her report to the U.S. Senate outlined the CIA torturing and brutality against detainees and in some cases death of detainees. Retired Colonel Lawrence Wilkinson Administrative Assistance to George W. Bush's Secretary of State Colin Powell stated that George W. Bush, Vice-President Dick Cheney, CIA Director George Tenet, Secretary of Defense Donald H. Rumsfeld, former Attorney –General Alberto Gonzales, and White House Attorney John Yoo all should be prosecuted for War Crimes. The CIA utilized the same methods of torturing and brutality as the Soviet Union KGB under Joseph Stalin did from 1924-1956. In his great book Gulag Archipelago Aleksandr Solzhenitsyn gave a graphic description of the torturing and inhuman brutality used by the KGB against political prisoners of the Soviet's State (A. Solzhenitsyn won the 1970 Noble Prize in Literature). All of the detainees that were being tortured by the CIA in their black sites were people of color. Inside the United States white police officers are killing unarmed brown and black people. The United States not only perpetrates racial hate crimes as a foreign policy also perpetrate crimes of racism against their own black and brown populations.

Igor Panarin a Russian's Scholar has predicted that the United States will break apart like the Soviet Union did in the 1980 because of its injustice and racial hate crimes against its diverse cultural and political ` populations.

President Obama was asked about the Grand juries failures to indict white police officers in New York and Ferguson, Missouri for killing unarmed black individuals. President Obama stated that the United States race problems goes back four hundred years. President Obama further stated that It would take many centuries to resolve the United States race problem.

SONY ENTERTAINMENT PROBLEMS WITH
NORTH KOREA REGARDING A MOVIE THE INTERVIEW

I have not seen the movie and I have no intention of seeing the movie. The North Korean's Representatives have alleged that the movie interview demeans, degrades, their leader Kim Jong Un and their country. The two producers who made the movie Interview Mr. Seth Rogen and Mr. Evan Goldberg are both Jewish individuals. Hollywood has for nearly a century made movies that degraded, demeaned Black, Brown, Native Americans, Asians, and Middle Eastern individuals without suffering any consequences. Hollywood has a history and culture which has perpetrated racial characterizations of people of color in the United States. Mr. Seth Rogen nor Mr. Evan Goldberg have never made any movies which demeans and degrades the Nation of Israel. Brown, Black, Asians, and native American people do not have nuclear weapons and the fourth largest army in the world like the North Koreans. Black, Brown, Asians, and Native Americans people do not have the power that the North Koreans possess to prevent the powerful Sony Hollywood producers from perpetrating demeaning and degrading characterizations of their Communities. Sony Entertainment at their top executive offices do not have the representation of persons of color. Mr. Scott Rudin Hollywood producer and Sony Pictures co-chairman Ms. Amy Pascal exchanged emails in which they made racially offensive jokes about President Obama. Further Mr. Scott Rudin made disparaging remarks about actress Ms. Angelina Jolie. Hollywood has been a racially prejudice culture toward people of color in the United States and people of color of African, Middle Eastern, Asian, (native American cultures).

BREAK UP OF THE AMERICAN EMPIRE

This scholar believes that the American Empire will break up like the Roman Empire of the fourth Century A.D. The United States is currently in the process of moral decade with men marrying men and women marrying women. Chief Justice of the United States Supreme Court John Roberts ruled that states' laws that denies people of the same sex from getting married is unconstitutional.

The United States Empire is militarily and economically over extended. The birth of the white population is not reproducing themselves as the rate of the non-white populations. There are more white people dying then there are babies being born to white women.

The Russian's Scholar Igor Panarin foresee the United States Empire falling in about twenty Years (2020 A.D.). People of color do not believe that they have access to equal to justice in the United States of America. The Grand Juries in New York and Ferguson, Missouri substantiate people of color believes that the American Criminal Justice System is racist system which denies them equal justice.

The United States after 9-11 the CIA according to the Senate Intelligence (Dianne Feinstein 's report) Committee report on the treatment of detainees after 9-11 attacks, members of a CIA interrogation team were "profoundly affected some to the point of tears and choking up at the brutality treatment In 2002 of an important Al-Quaida detainee named Abu Zubaida.

Captured in Pakistan and taken to a secret facility in Thailand, zubaida was initially cooperative, willingly providing answers under normal, on-coercive questioning. But the CIA abruptly halted his interrogation, placed him in isolation for 47 days and began a regime of astonishing and gratuitous cruelty (Aleksandr Solzhenitsyn, Gulag Archipelago, 1970, Noble prize).

Torturers slammed him against walls, confined him in coffin-size boxes for a total of nearly 300 hours and subjected him to 83 sessions of water boarding, which simulated drowning, a practice for which Japanese war criminals were tried, convicted and harshly punished following World War II.

The Senate report cites the high-profile case of Khalid Al-Masri, a Lebanese man living in Germany who was grabbed in 2003 by Macedonian authorities and handed over to U.S. officials on erroneous suspicions of terrorist ties. Al-Masri was flown to the Salt Pit, where he was subjected to abusive interrogation tactics and held for months until his captors turned him loosen an Albanian road April 2004. He sued the U.S government unsuccessfully in American courts but won compensation from Macedonia in a 2012 judgment by the European Court of Human rights (The United nations has held that the U.S. utilize racial profiling and the U.S Criminal Justice System perpetrate injustice against Black and Brown people in the U.S.U.N. Report, 2014).

Nikita Khrushchev (April 15,1894 to Sep. 11,1971) became the Soviet Premier in 1956 after the death of Joseph Stalin and Khrushchev allow the Soviet 's people and openness to discuss the crime against the people and the Soviet State committed by Stalin from 1924 to Stalin's death in 1956. Senate Dianne Feinstein stated in her releasing the CIA report that the U.S. was unique that its allowed its' crimes to be released to the world. Khrushchev in 1956 allowed the crimes of Stalin to be released to the Soviet's people and to the world.

PRESIDENT OBAMA MADE HISTORY IN DIPLOMATIC
CHANGE IN RELATIONSHIP WITH FIDEL CASTRO CUBA

President Obama ended a fifty years of hostility between the People Republic of Cuba and the United States in 2014. Fidel Castro led a rebellion against the Cuban dictator Fulgencio Batista in 1957. Batista was supported by the United States. U.S. corporation owned nearly 90 percent of the Cuban's economy and all their natural resources. The non-white Cubans were practically slaves to the U.S. and the Cuban white ruling class. During the fifties the U.S. was a racially segregated society. All African-Americans lived in total racial oppression. The United States Senate from Florida Mr. Marco Rubio represents the white Cubans that Castro driven out of Cuban when he seized the Cuban 's Government in 1957. African-Americans have a great deal of affection for Fidel Castro because the Cuban's Army defeated the White South African Army in Angelo, African War of 1987-1988. The Cuban's Army defeated the White South African's Army at an Angelo Village called Cuito Cuanavale in 1988. The White South African-Army was supported by the United States and the country of Israel.

The African-American population in the United States do not believe that the U.S. will grant them full political and equal rights under the U.S. Constitution of 1787. The African-American population have been in America since arriving in Virginia in 1619. The U.S. attempted to grant African-Americans equal rights in the passage of the 1964 Civil Rights Act by Lyndon B. Johnson.

The campaign to grant Black people the rights under the U.S. constitution that the white population enjoy has failed. Russia under Czar Alexander II attempted to grant rights to the Russian's peasants in the Great Reform Act of 1872 also failed. The A Romans attempted to grant Roman's rights to the German tribes also failed. The Soviet Union attempted to grant rights to countries and cultures under its domination in Eastern Europe also failed. Israel continue their oppression of Arab populations in Israel and the criminal occupation of the Palestinians in Gaza.

African-Americans of my generation an age are afraid to drive our cars in fear of the white police officers will racially profile and shoot and kill us without justification (Michael Brown, Ferguson, Missouri, Eric Garner in New York, Rodney King 1991, in Los Angeles).

I believe that the U.S. is on a historical course of break-up like the Soviet Empire and all other empires of world history. Citizens of color do not believe that they have the same rights under the U.S. constitution as the U.S. white citizens. Citizens of color do not believe that they have rights under the U.S. constitution. The U.S. will have to utilize the police to maintain order in the U.S. cities.

President Abraham Lincoln (1809-1865) the sixteenth United States president stated" "That force is all conquering, but its victories are short lived." We are living at the end of the United States Empire and the rise of the Chinese Empire. The Roman's Republic begin in 509 B.C. The Roman's Republic ended when Augustus Caesar became the Emperor and ruling from 27 B.C to his death at 14 A.D. The Roman Empire became repressive externally and internally.

The American Empire begin as a Democracy with the Founding Father creating the Constitution on 1787, however imperfect (slavery). The American Empire ended with the defeat of George W. Bush in Iraq and Afghanistan. The American Empire after the attack on 9-11 begin a campaign of repression internally with the Patriot Act and externally with CIA torturing, and water boarding detainees (2003-2008, Dianne Feinstein's Senate Report on 2014, Howard Zinn, A People History of United States 1980, 1492-Present, Harper and Row, Harper Collins, 1980).

AMERICAN REPLACE NAZIS GERMANY AS NORDIC RACIST EMPIRE in 1945

Was the American the ideal country of democracy during World War II. Did the U.S. Respect the rights of minorities in the U.S. In 1941 when the U.S. entered the War against Germany and Japan was a racist apartheid country that oppressed black people, Asian People And Native American People. The U.S. step forward as the defenders of helpless countries matched its image in American high school history textbooks, but not its record in world affairs. The U.S. had opposed the Haiti revolution for independence from France at the start of the Nineteenth century (Thomas Jefferson as the U.S. President refused to support the People Haitia Independence from France, 1807). The U.S. was a slave civilization and the Jefferson's Government refused to support black people in their struggle against France 's oppression and slavery Haiti.

The U.S. instigated a war with Mexico and taken half of their country for the specific purpose Of expanding the institution of slavery to the new acquired territories, (California, New Mexico, Colorado, Utah, and Texas). U.S presented to help Cuba after the Spanish American War of 1898. The little island of Cuba had gone through a revolution in 1959 led by Fidel Castro. The U.S. backed the their American's dictator Fulgencio Batista. The revolution was backed by American business's interest who owned 99% of the Cuban's wealth. American's businesses owned 100% percent of Cub's utilities, mines, cattle ranches, and oil refineries, 40 percent of the sugar industries, and 50 percent of the public railways. In fact American's companies owned the entire island of Cuba After the Spanish American War of 1898. The U.S. seized Hawaii and made the Hawaiian People slaves in their own country. After the Spanish American War of 1898 the U.S. seized Puerto Rico, Guam, and fought a brutal war to subjugate the Filipinos People. The War with the Filipino Insurgents was a war that included water boarding by the U.S. troops during the Filipino War of 1898-1901.

The U.S. engaged in an Open door foreign policy toward China with the other European Powers, Germany, United Kingdom, France, and Japan. The U.S. was among the European Powers that was engaged in the opioid trade in China after the Opium War of 1832-1842. American's business men made a great profit in the opioda trade in China. The U.S. sent troops to China during the Open Door Policy to protect their businesses in 1900.

The U.S. sent a naval armada to Japan in 1854 to force the Japanese to open their ports to the U.S. for trade through the threat of military invasion. The U.S. engineered a revolution against Colombia and created an independence state of Panama in order to build and control the Panama Canal. In 1926 sent five thousands troops to Nicaragua to prevent the people of Nicaragua from obtaining their human rights and kept their troops there for seven years. The U.S. intervened in the Dominican Republic and kept U.S. troops there for eight years to protect the U.S. companies interest. The U.S. intervened in Honduras seven times to protect the interest of American's companies that owned 99 percent of all of the natural resources of the country.

Just before the World War I ended, in 1918 an American force of seven thousand landed at Vladivostok as part of an allied intervention in Russia to assist the Loyalist forces of the deposed Czar of Russia to fight the Communist forces of Nicholas Lenin. The U.S. all way fought on the side of countries that were engaged in the racist oppression of poor people of color all over the world(U.S. and the State of Israel provided financial and military support of the racist Government of South Africa Against Nelson Mandela and the African National Congress). Between 1900 and 1933 the U.S. intervened in Cuba four times, in Nicaragua twice, in Panama six times, in Guatemala once, in Honduras seven times. By 1924 the finances of half of the twenty Latin American states were being directed by the United States. In Guatemala, in 1954, a legally elected government was overthrown by an invasion force of mercenaries trained and directed by the CIA in military bases in Honduras and Nicaragua planes flown by American's CIA officers. The invasion put in power Colonel Carlos Castillo Armas a military dictator Armed and supported by the U.S. Government with the direction of the CIA. The Government That the U.S. overthrew was the most democratic Guatemala had ever had. The President Jacobo Arbenz, was a left-socialist. President Arbenz was going to nationalize U.S. Fruit Company which owned 99 percent of all of the agricultural land in Guatemala. Arbenz Promised the poor people in Guatemala that he would provide them with their own lands to farm. The United Fruit Company secured the cooperation of the CIA and they overthrown a Democratic election President to secure the agricultural lands for the U.S. company the United Fruit company. All of the poor pheasants in Guatemala were enslaved by the U.S. CIA and the United Fruit Company to indefinite servitude as slaves in their own country.

The CI At trained the secret police of Colonel Carlos Castillo Armas on methods of torture and Water boarding of poor Guatemala's people who opposed the dictatorship of the U.S. Selected strongman Carlos Castillo Armas. The U.S. Secretary of State John Foster Dulles And his brother Allen Dulles Director of the CIA was given stocks by the United Fruit Company for their overthrowing the Democratic elected Guatemala's President Jacobo Arbenz in 1954. In 1959 The Cuban's revolutionary leader Fidel Castro was threatening The U.S. dictator Fulgencio Batista who was placed in power in Cuba to protect the interest Of U.S. corporations by the U.S. government and the CIA. The U.S. obtained the military Control of Cuba as a result of the Spanish

American War of 1898. U.S. corporations owned 99 percent of All of the natural resources of the Cuba. The non-white population of Cuba segregated and racially Oppressed like the non-white people of color in the U.S. home land. Everywhere the American white People went they oppressed people of color all over the U.S. empire (Cuba, Nicaragua, Honduras, Chile, Panama, Mexico, El Salvador, Hawaii, Guam, Africa, and Asia). During World War II the U.S. was a racist apartheid nation with people of color existing in absolute racist oppression and subjected to a government that was committed to their absolute oppression. When the second World War was being fought as a result of Adolphe Hitler's Government was wrong in his ideas of Germany's racial superiority or white Nordic supremacy the U.S. was a country who ideas of white racial superiority was more dominant than Hitler's Empire. The U.S. promoted the ideas that U.S. citizens of color was inferior to the U.S. white population. When troops were jammed onto the Queen Mary in early 1945 to go to combat duty in the European theater ; the blacks were stowed down in the depths of the ship near the engine room, as far as possible from fresh air of the deck, in bizarre reminder of the slave voyages of old (Jewish's businesses made a great deal of money in the African-slave trade. Monsanto a Jewish's company was a slave trading company in the 15th and 16th centuries and after slavery came to an end after the American's Civil War1861-1865 Monsanto changed from a slave trading company to a drug producer).

The Red Cross, with U.S. government approval, separated the blood donations of black and white soldiers during the War and all U.S. hospitals and medical centers in U.S. Dr. Charles Drew an African-American doctor invented the process of preserving blood which saved millions of American soldiers during World War II. Dr. Drew was injury in an automobile accident in the U.S. South. The closest white hospital would not provide him medical care because he was black. Dr. Drew died as a result of not being provided immediate medical care by the all white hospital. When the U.S. declared war on Germany in 1941 the U.S. was a racist segregated country that denied All of their Constitutional rights to all persons of color in the United States. In the American's South the white supremacy were lynching African-American 6,000 annually. African-Americans were denied educationally, job, and in many legal jurisdiction black people could not serve on juries and the criminal justice and prison systems were racist repressive against all people of color. Black people and other people of color existed in absolute fear of white hatred and extermination. All people of color were subjected to racial extermination, genocide, and holocaust.

German's government officials came to the U.S. to study the American's Indian's Reservations Systems (the incarceration Native People on Reservation which led to extermination, and genocide of Native People, Buried My Heart At Wounded Knee, 1970, Dee Brown). The German's Government officials went back to Germany and established their system of Concentrations through Europe (incarceration of Jews, political prisoners, and people of Eastern European for extermination by the SS Nazis Guards, 1939-1945). In Buck V.Bell, 274,U.S., 200 (1927), was a decision of the U.S. supreme court, written by Justice Oliver Wendell Homes, Jr., in which the court ruled that states' statutes that permitted compulsory sterilization of the unfit, including the intellectually disable, for the protection and health of the state did not violate the Due Process Clause of the 14th Amendment. All states' jurisdictions could use compulsory sterilization on the disable, mentally unfit, people of color, black, brown, and Asian people (U.S. government provided funds to state's government for sterilization of mentally unfit, disable, and intellectually persons, and Latino women for sterilization, Madrigal V. Quilligan, 1978, a District Court decision which mandated hat all people had to have consent forms in their primary language. Los Angeles USC Medical Center was sterilizing Latino women who could not speak English was providing them with Consent forms for sterilization in English. The USC was not sterilizing white women they were only sterilizing Latino women). After World War II the German's Nazis doctors who were on trial in 1946 used in their defense that they obtained their methods of racial extermination, sterilization from the U.S. methods of racial extermination and sterilization of people of color, the disable, mentally and intellectually unfit in Buck V. Bell, 1927, U.S. Supreme Court Decision of compulsory sterilization. The U.S. claims of democracy, human rights was not nothing but racist mythology of the American's empire (Nick Turse, Kill Everything that Moves, 2010, Vietnam War, crimes). George W. Bush, Dick Cheney, Donald Rumsfeld, illegally invaded Iraq in 2003 are wanted by The International Court at Hague for War Crimes during the Iraq War 2003-2008.

The creation of the United nations during the war was presented to the world as international Cooperation to prevent future wars. But the U.N. was dominated by the Western imperial powers, With military bases and power and influence in Eastern European by the Russia. Republican U.S. Senator Arthur Vandenburg stated that the U.N. was a tool by which U.S. corporations could maintain imperialist control of the world after the Second World War, 1939-1945. The U.N. was established by the U.S. for the specific purpose of dominating the world's economies. (Zinn, Howard, A People's History of the United States, P. 415, Harper Collins). The European powers that won the second World War were concerned about maintaining The economic dominance of their empires (French Indo-china, British Empire in Asia, U.S. Pacific Empire and the Middle Oil for their oil companies (Iran, Saud-Arabia). The U. S. their country as a defender of human rights. The U.S. has been the greatest violate of Human rights all over the world and the U.S. Empire. When the Japanese attacked Pearl Harbor There was anti-Japanese hatred toward Japanese-Americans. One American Congressman said " I am for catching every Japanese in America, Alaska and Hawaii now putting them in concentration Camps, Dam them, Let get rid of them." (Zinn Howard, A People's History of the United States, p. 416,Harpers Collins Publishers, 1999). President Franklin D. Roosevelt did not share in the hatred of Japanese-Americans, but he signed Executive Order 9066 for the incarceration of Japanese – American up in concentration camps throughout the United States. In 1944 the Supreme Court upheld the forced evacuation on the grounds of military necessity (American's Concentration camps, Arkansas, Arizona, Colorado, Utah, Idaho, Wyoming, and California). In 1836 The U.S. congress Passed the Great India Removal Acts and President Andrew Jackson removed the Native People From their lands in Georgia and Tennessee for their lands and place the Native People in Concentration Camps in the Oklahoma Territories (the Trial of Tears 1836, Native People women were raped, and killed by U.S. Troops during the long journey, Buried My Heart At Wounded Knee, Dee Brown, 1970).

The United States dropped the atom bombs on Japan on August 6, and 9 of 1945 was unnecessary The Japanese 's government had contacted the Russian's government asked to communicate With the U.S. that they were ready to negotiate a peace treaty to end the war in the Pacific. General George Marshall recommended to the U.S. government to provide the Japanese's Government a warning before the U.S. dropped the atom bombs. The U.S. government and the U.S. Military want to dropped the bombs on Hiroshima and Nagasaki for the specific purpose of Killing hundreds of thousands of Japanese people (During the Vietnam War 1964-1975 the U.S. killed Over 5 millions Vietnamese civilians, Nick Turse, Kill Everything that Moves, Search and Destroy). The U.S. in 1945 was the greatest economic power in world. The U.S. had an Open Door Policy Which means that the U.S. empire was going to replace the British's Empire in ruling the world. The U.S. in 1945 moved into the Middle East for the specific purpose of seizing all of the oil In Syria, Iraq, Saudi Arabia and suppressing and supporting the creation of the State of Israel as a white European colony in the Middle East. The U.S. and Israel became the primary military and economic supporters of the White Racist Government of South Africa. In 1953 the U.S. and Great Britain conspired in the overthrowal of the democratic elected president of Iran Mohammod Mossadegah. The British company of Anglo-Iranian Oil company controlled 98 percent of the Iranian's People oil resources. Mossadegah was elected in 1953 and begin nationalizing the British's Anglo-Iranian Oil company. The British's Intelligence contacted the CIA Director John foster Dulles and they conspired and overthrown the Democratic elected Iranian's government under Mossadegah.

The current problems in the Middle East was caused by the U.S. economic, military campaign to seize the Arab's people natural resources of oil in the Middle East (The U.S. exterminated Native American People for the specific purpose of seizing the lands and natural resources 1862-1890 Wounded Knee Massacre, Buried My heart At Wounded Knee, 1970, Dee Brown). The U.S. support of the white people in Israel is the U.S. need a colony of white people in the Middle East to assist the U.S. in their campaign to control the oil resources in the Middle East (Balfour Declaration, 1917). At the end of World War II American's Corporations controlled the U.S. government. The U.S. Empire is a corporation controlled and ran by U.S. corporations and the U.S. military defense companies. The American's Civilization and the capitalist system was built by African-American slaves, Asian's Slaves workers built the

Intercontinental Rail Roads, and Latino-laborers built the U.S. agricultural dominance in the world (U.S. Constitution 1787, legalized slavery, Article IV, Section 1, Provision 3 made black people property, 1857 Dred Scott's Decision, racist slave owner chief Justice Roger B. Taney from North Carolina ruled that black People were property, not citizen of U.S.). African-American slaves built the white House, Washington Mall, and Lady Liberty on top of the Capital). The American's Empire was built by slave laborers for a white racist apartheid civilization.

President Donald Trump was elected president in 2016. Trump did not create American's Racism. Adolphe Hitler did not create ant-Semitism in 1933. The hatred of Jews had existed In European civilization thousands for years. Hitler and Trump just took advantage of the hatred to advance their political careers. A majority of all of the American's President took advantage of the American's white population racist hatred toward their non-white population to advance their political careers (Washington, Jefferson, Ronald Reagan, G.H.Bush, G W. Bush, Bill Clinton (Crime bill,, War on drugs), and President Donald Trump).

PRESIDENT TRUMP MIGRANT CARAVAN
FROM CENTRAL AND SOUTH AMERICA

President Donald Trump did not create the immigrant problems on our borders. The Problems on the U.S borders were created by the U.S. government and U.S. corporation and the CIA. The U.S. intervention in South America begin with their support of the French in their military Campaign to suppress the Haitian's people rebellion against their French colonial occupation In August 22,1791. The French like the British had established colonies all throughout the New World. The French had their own people established on the Island of Haiti from France. The French's had very successful Sugar Plantations producing sugar and rum for consumption through our the North American colonies. The French made a great deal of money from the Sugar Plantations in what The French called Saint Domingue. The French had brought over black slave from African as Laborers to work the Sugar Plantations. The American Colonies had also introduced slavery In their colonies in

1619. When the enslaved black people in Haiti rebelled against their French enslavers in Saint Domingue on August 22,1791 the U.S. had just ended their Revolutionary War against the British Empire on 1778. All of the U.S. Founding Fathers were owners of a large slave population on their plantations (George Washington, Thomas Jefferson, James Madison, James Monroe, and Andrew Jackson). The New U.S. Republic was a racist slave nation and they Were committed to protecting the institution of slavery. The new republic was so committed to Protecting slavery they wrote provisions in their new Constitution of 1787 to protect their rights to protect their institution of slavery. In the their new Constitution of 1787, Article IV, Section 1, provision 3, was placed in the new Constitution to ensure that the Founding Fathers protected their property rights to own slaves. The New U.S. slave Republic encouraged and supported the French's Government in their military campaign to destroy the new Haitian Independence in 1791-1803. In 1811 there was a slave rebellion in Louisiana. The rebellion was led by Charles Delondes a slave that had arrived from Haiti. President Jefferson had purchased Louisiana from the French in 1807. President Thomas Jefferson used the U.S. Army to put down the slave rebellion In Louisiana very brutally. The U.S. Arm and the people of the Louisiana was very brutal in putting down The slave rebellion. The U.S. had to make an example of the slaves who had rebelled. The New U.S. Republic was a slave nation with millions of African People their legal slave institution.

In 1823 James Monroe who was President after Thomas Jefferson owned slaves on his plantation. James Monroe established the Monroe Doctrine in 1823 which established that South America, Central America was no longer open for European colonialization. The U.S. begin a campaign of Intervention in all of the South American and Central American countries to seize their natural resources and enslaving all of people of color in the new world.

In 1954, the CIA helped orchestrate the overthrow of a democratically elected government In Guatemala. A U.S. corporation the United Fruit company owned 98 percent of all of the Agricultural lands in Guatemala. In 1954 the new democratically elected president of Guatemala Jacobo Arbenz begin nationalizing the land and property of the United Fruit company. The CIA with the approval of President Eisenhower orchestrated the overthrowal President Arbenz. The CIA begin training the secret police of the CIA's dictator

Colonel Carlos Castillo Armas in his campaign to suppress the poor people of Guatemala.. The United Fruit Company rewarded the U.S. CIA director with stocks from their company for his efforts in overthrowing Guatemala's President Arbenz in 1954. In the Cuban's revolution of 1959 the CIA again supported their Dictator Fulgencio Batista against the forces of Fidel Castro. The CIA attempted to kill Castro to prevent him from nationalizing the property of U.S. corporations that owned 99 percent of all of the Cuban's natural resources. The U.S. population and government had introduced their policy of racial apartheid into their new acquired colony of Cuba. Black Cuban were completely racially oppressed by the U.S. government and the their white population that vacation in Cuba. When Castro came to power he nationalized the property of the U.S. corporation and he provide Human rights to the black Cuban people (Black people in the U.S. was completed oppressed).

THE CIA COUP IN CHILE IN 1973
BY PRESIDENT NIXON AND HENRY KISSINGER

The CIA orchestrated a campaign to overthrow a democratically elected government of Salvador Allende in 1973. President Allende stated that he going to nationalize the property of U.S. Corporations in Chile. The people of Chile were existing in absolute poverty while the dependents of U.S. corporations that resided in Chile lived like kings and queens. The U.S. had transplanted their racism and racist hate of people of color to the people of Chile. The white racist Henry Kissinger who was President Nixon Secretary of State encouraged and supported the new Chile's dictator Augusto Pinochet (Henry Kissinger was indicted for War Crimes by the International Court for his murdering of millions of Vietnamese people in the Vietnam War 1964-1975). The U.S. CIA Director during the campaign to overthrow Chile President Salvador Allende was Richard Helm. The CIA trained dictator Augusto Pinochet's secret police in the techniques of water boarding, torture, and all kinds of inhuman torturing (Gina Haspel new female director of CIA ran a CIA torturing center in Thailand during the George W. Bush's Administration 2003-2008).

The current problems with the refugees at the U.S. borders were created by the policies of the CIA, U.S. corporations, and the American Presidents for the specific purpose of seizing all of the natural resources of South and Central American Governments. The U.S. Government has overthrown democratically elected in South and Central America since the Monroe Doctrine in 1823. The U.S. conspired to invade and Mexico in 1846 for the specific purpose of seizing Mexican's territories of California, Utah, Colorado, Arizona, and New Mexico. President Polk Was a Southern and he wanted to expand slavery and he need new territories for Southern slave holders. The American imperialist were promoting and supporting the Manifest Destiny position. The Manifest Destiny was an imperialist position that the U.S. should expand from Atlantic Ocean to the Pacific Ocean. President Polk ordered U.S. troops in Mexican's territory and he went United States Congress and claimed that Mexico had attacked U.S. troops in American's territory. Abraham Lincoln was a Senator from Illinois and he opposed the declaration of war against Mexico. Lincoln stated that he believed that President Polk was involved in a conspiracy with Southern slave owners to expand slavery in the United States.

The Pentagon Papers' proved that the Gulf of Tonkin resolution which was a fake attack on the A U.S. Warship the Maddox did not happen. The Johnson's Administration had made up the entire Incident that the North Vietnamese had attacked the Maddox in International waters was a fake story for the purpose of introducing U.S. troops into the Vietnam conflict. George W. Bush created the fake story about Saddam Hussein had nuclear bombs. The Iraq's President did not have nuclear weapons. The Bush's Administration made up the story for the purpose of invading the country of Iraq. George W. Bush and his confederates were planning the Iraq War for two years before the 9-11 World Tower occurred. Bush was meeting with representatives from U.S. oil corporations for the specific purpose developing plans for the dividing up of the Iraq's reserves. In 1939 Adolphe Hitler arranged for German's soldiers to be dressed up as polish's soldiers and seized a German's radio station and to disseminate anti-German information. Hitler and his confederates claimed that Poland had attack Germany's territory and Hitler went to the German's Parliament and requested a declaration of war against Poland. Hitler invasion of Poland in 1939 begun the Second World War. Hitler's purpose for invading Poland was for the Polish's land and natural resources which Germany lacked.

President Donald Trump meeting with the North Korean Leader Kim Jong Un in 2018 and 2019 Was not unusual for American's Presidents. Since World War 11 all of the American's Presidents Have encouraged and supported dictators all throughout south and Central American (1954 overthrown Guatemala democratically elected President and CIA replaced Arbenz with the dictator Carlos Castillo Armas, in 1973 the CIA overthrown Chile's democratically elected president Salvador Allende and replaced him with their dictator Augusto Pinochet, 1953 the CIA Overthrown Iran's democratically elected President Mohammad Mossadegh and replaced him With the Shah of Iran. The CIA trained the Shah's secret police in the methods of waterboarding and other methods of inhuman torturing of Iranian people). President Nixon approved the overthrowing of Chile's President Allende in 1973 and President Eisenhower approved the CIA overthrowing the Iranian's President Mossadegh and the President of Guatemala's Jacobo Arbenz in 1954 for the American Company United Fruit company. President Trump made history by meeting with the North Korean's President Kim Jong Un In 2018 and 2019. President's meetings had the effect of reducing the chance of nuclear war with North Korea. Mr. Trump meetings with the North Korean's President Kim Jong Un has open up opportunities for him and future U.S. Presidents to negotiate with the North Korean's President. Mr. Trump in his political campaigns used race as a rallying tools for his supporters have been Used by other politicians. Adolphe Hitler used race to win the German's chancellorship in1939 And Presidents George H. W. Bush used Willie Horton (poor black) to rally his base in the 1984 Presidential campaign against his Democratic opposition. Bill Clinton used the Crime bill and War on Crime to get elected in 1990. President Ronald Reagan also used race as a tool to win his Election in 1980 against President Jimmy Carter. Reagan obtained the total support of the Southern White Religious Right to win his election in 1980. Donald Trump use of race to win his election was not a rear incident since other Presidents had used race as a political tool to win the presidency.

WILL RACE, CULTURE, AND TRIBISM
CAUSED POLITICAL DIVISION OF U.S. EMPIRE

President Donald Trump used racial prejudice to win the American's President in 2016. Adolphe Hitler also used racial prejudice against Jews and the other to win the German's Chancellorship in 1939. Several of the U.S. President's candidates used racial prejudice to Win the U.S. Presidency (Woodrow Wilson, Ronald Reagan, George H.W. Bush, Bill Clinton, and Donald Trump). President Trump used racism to unite his supporters And obtain the Presidency in 2016. Former President Ronald Reagan was able to Obtain the support of the Klu Klux Klan in his 1980 political campaign for the Presidency Over President Jimmy Carter. President George H.W. bush used the story of the Willie Horton. Willie Horton was a poor black man who had been placed on probation and While on probation committed another crime. Bill Clinton used the fear of crime by promising White people that he was going to touch on crime. The racist implication was that all black men Were criminals. Clinton started the mass incarceration of men of color and the institution of the private prison system in the United States. The United States is a extremely racially polarized civilization. The racial polarization begin with the Founding Fathers when they formed the American Republic in 1787 at the Constitution Convention in 1787. The founding Fathers were all slave holders and they placed a provision in the 1787 Constitution to protect their property rights to own African-American slaves. The U.S. fought a Civil War from 1861-1865 to end the night mare of institutional slavery in American. The American Civil War did not end racism in the United States. Black People have been in the U.S. since 1619 over 400 hundreds years. The U.S. was built on the philosophy of the superiority of the white race. The American's empire like their cousin the British Empire was also built on the philosophy of the superiority of the white race. Adolphe Hitler established his empire on the concept of the racial superiority of the white German race. The Roman empire was also based on the superiority of the Roman's race. The Spanish Empire was also built on the theory of the racial superiority of the Spanish white race. All of the white European empires were built on the racial superiority of their white race over all of the people of color of Africa, Asia, and all people of color in the new World during the 16th and 20th centuries. World War One was about the European Powers dominance of the people of color throughout their empires in Asia, Africa, and in Central and South America. The U.S. Empire was built totally by slave laborers (White House, Washington Mall, Transcontinental Rail road was built by Chinese slave laborers). California had race riots in 1871 in Los Angeles and San Francisco against Chinese People where there were hundreds of Chinese People were killed during those killing sprees by racist angry white people. The U.S. Republic was built clearly on white racist hatred toward people of color in the U.S. The U.S. Capitalist system was built by slave laborers and people of color. The U.S. is the only empire in the world where their democracy was build on the backs of slave laborers.

The U.S. African-America population are currently being subjected to police brutality, racial Profiling, racist criminal justice system, privatization of the U.S. prison system, (Furman V. George, 1972, black and brown men were targeted for death penalty as a result of their race). Brown People in the U.S. are being targeted by President Trump for incarceration, and racist Concentration camps as a result of their race (Adolphe Hitler rounded up people who Were racially different for their concentration camps, 1939-1945). white journalists on the fox News channel alleging the Brown people are committing all of the crimes in America. All of the Mass Killers in the U.S. are white males (Las Vega, Borderline café in thousands Oaks, California).

The history of civilizations and empires support the theory that all empires break up the people of that empire divide up into group, race, tribes, and cultures when the Empire decline and fall (Greek Empire after the death of Alexander the Great 323 B.C., Roman empire 476 A.D., The Spanish Empire after the Spanish American War of 1898, The British Empire after the Second World War, The Russian Empire after the Russian revolution of 1917, and the U.S. Empire after their defeat in Vietnam, Iraq, Syria, and Afghanistan 2003-2009). President Trump is symbolic of the decline of the American Empire. The Chinese Empire will and have replaced the U.S. Empire. President Trump represent the immoral depravity of the American ruling class. Racism is the disease that is leading to the destruction of the U.S. Empire from within. The Soviet Union declined as a result of their military campaign in Afghanistan in 1987. The Soviet Union dominated Eastern European as a result of conquering and occupying all of the countries of Eastern European after the Second World War. In 1989 the countries of Eastern Europe begin to demanding the freedom from the Soviet 's Empire. The Soviet Empire had become economically weak from the long military campaign in Afghanistan.

The U.S. Empire like the Soviet's Empire has been involved in a long wars in Iraq and Afghanistan and the U.S. Empire was defeated in their military adventures in the Middle East. The British and the Soviet Union were defeated in their military campaigns in Afghanistan. President George W. Bush invaded Iraq in 2003 for the specific purpose of seizing the Iraq's Oil reserves was defeated by the Iraq's insurgents who were defending their country and their way of life. George W. Bush's military campaign in Iraq the U.S. troop, and Air Force killed over a million Iraq's civilians. George W. bush approved and supported the torturing of Iraq's prisoners and Iraq's citizens who were non-combatants (Gina Haspel, first woman Director of CIA supervised a torturing unit in Thailand.2003-2008).

The new U.S. Republic beginning in 1787 was not a democracy. The Founding Fathers In their philosophy for developing a democracy studied the ancient history of the Greek city State of Athens. Ancient Athens in the time of Plato in 400 B.C. had 2 million people. Ancient Athens was a slave state. There were only forty thousands people who had the right to participate in the privileges of the Athenian's State. A majority of the Athenian's population were slaves, foreigners, and traders. Ancient Athens was clearly an oligarchy not a democracy. The American's Founding Fathers in 1787 at the Constitutional Convention in Philadelphia established and oligarchy of a slavery republic. All of the founding Fathers were owners of thousands of African People as slaves on their plantations. The new Constitution of 1787 legalized slavery (Article IV, Section 1, Provision 3). The American Revolution was not about freedom. The American Revolution was about the property class was angry about having to send their products to England. They were losing money by sending all of the agricultural products to England at low price and they could make more money by selling their products directly to France and receive more profit. The American's Revolution was clearly about profit not freedom. The British in a famous case in the English's court was going to make slavery illegal in the British's Empire. The Founding Fathers who were all owners of a large slave population. The Founding Fathers were afraid that they were going to have to give up their property which were African slaves. North American English colonies were established by British's Corporations. The East Indian Company (Controlled the opium trade in China 1832-1842 Opium War)., South Sea Company, and the Virginia Company. The colonization of North American was a commercial venture by the British's Corporations. All of the people the British shipped over to North American were the undesirable people that the British wanted throw away. The British's people who were doing well did not leave England. The British established South Carolina and Georgia as prison colonies for their criminal's populations. (Australia was originally a prison colony for British's criminals). The British's corporation made massive profits in their establishing North American colonies. Britain, France, Russia, and China were countries that were established by people desiring home for their families not generating profit. The new American Republic was established for the specific purpose of making profit by the British's Corporations(Dickerson, James, Inside America's Concentration Camps, p. 15, 2010). The American's Constitution of 1787 was established for the specific purpose protecting the rights and privileges of the American ruling class the founding Fathers. The Constitution did not grant rights to vote to white males that did not own property. The right to vote was only granted to white males that owned property. Poor white men in Britain in 1787 did not have the right to vote. The right to vote was granted only to white men who owned property in the England's colonies in 1787. The Founding Fathers did not grant the rights to vote to white women, Native -Americans, Nor people of color including black people from African. The new American Republic was clearly an oligarchy of property owning rich white men. The American of President Donald Trump is an American owned by Corporations and ruled by an oligarchy of rich white men. All of the American's Presidents beginning with George Washington were owned and controlled by the rich property owning class in the U.S. The rich property owning class told the lower class white men that they were racially superior to the non-white people. People by nature would like to believe that their tribe is superior to another race or tribe of people. The white European civilizations begin in the 16 Century to conquer non-white civilizations and they promoted White European superiority over non-white people they had conquered. The New American's Republic established white racial supremacy in their new 1787 Constitution. The white people in South African fought the African Congress of Nelson Mandela to keep their white privileges and racial supremacy in place in South African (The U.S. Government through CIA encouraged and supported the racial South African Government against Nelson Mandela and the African Congress struggle for freedom 1987-1994). The State of Israeli and the U.S. governments both encouraged and supported the white racist government in South African against Nelson Mandela and his freedom fighters.

The American white people in the U.S. are becoming a minority like the white people in South Africa. The American's white power structure are placing all of their white leaders in position of power. They are establishing themselves in control of the judiciary and the police departments throughout the United States. White Southern Politicians are using all kinds of methods to prevent black southern people from voting. The U.S. Criminal Justice System is subjecting black and brown people to an orchestrated campaign or organized racist hatred, police profiling, and systematic executions on the streets of America. In every American jurisdictions throughout the U.S. police departments are murdering black and brown people at an alarming rate. The U.S. has the largest prison population then any country in the world. A large number of the Inmates in U.S. prisons are people of color (South African's Prisons populations were a Majority of black people). The white males population in the U.S. are arming themselves in what they see is the coming race war in the U.S. White supremacy national groups are arming themselves and threatening the government and people of color.

Since the election of President Trump there have been an increase in white hate groups. President Trump did not create U.S. racism. The founding Fathers established racism in American in 1787 with new Constitution. The U.S. foreign policy since World War 11 has been a campaign of killing non-white people all over the world (Atomic Wars dropped on Japan, Vietnam War, torturing by CIA in Thailand, Syria, Afghanistan, and Iraq War). The U.S. police departments in all jurisdictions carry on a campaign of racist killing of black and brown men (Furman V. Georgia, 1972) daily throughout the U.S.

The U.S. empire has reached point that the Empire is declining as a result of immorality, Sexually depravity (Trump bizarre sexually habits) and homo sexuality in Hollywood, And the femininity among American white men (Homosexuality and femininity was a major caused of the decline of the Roman Empire). Rome had reached a major problem with recruiting soldiers for the roman's Army. The Roman had to recruit soldiers from their enemy the German's tribes. Rome's males had become to feminine to make soldiers. The rich's Roman men refused to join the army (Roman's Legion). Presidents Trump, George W. Bush, Mitt Romney, Vice -President Dick Cheney, President Theodore Roosevelt's father James Roosevelt hired a poor Irish man to take his place in the U.S. during the Civil War. All of these rich white men used their white privilege to avoid serving during war times in the America's Army. In American currently military recruiters are visiting high schools throughout America to recruit Black and brown young people for the U.S. imperialist army to kill black and brown people all over the World (Syria, Iraq, Afghanistan, Vietnam).

The break up of the American's empire will not implode today, but it will gradually break up Like all of the world empires. The historical signs of decade are apparent in the U.S. empire. The Rome reached a point that they could not afford to have an army all over the empire. The U.S. Empire cannot be sustained by poor people paying taxes while the rich people like President Trump avoid paying their fair share of the tax burden. President Trump treatment of the immigrants that are appearing at the U.S. borders are the creation of the U.S. economic and military and polices in Central and South America. The U.S. encouraged supported dictators throughout all Central and South America for U.S. corporations (Guatemala United Fruit company, 1954 CIA overthrown a democratically elected governments, Chile 1973 Cuba 1959 Castor's government, Reagan support contras in Nicaragua in 1980-81, and CIA training murders, and killers in El Salvador. All of the people of color in the U.S. do not believe in the U.S. philosophy of democracy. The concept of democracy was only a giant lie. People of color will never have the same rights as the U.S. white population. Racist conflicts will increase in the U.S. as a result of the decline in the white population. American fall will be internal not external fall. The Roman Empire fell internally when the German tribes arrived at the gates of Rome the Empire was already gone from internal decade, immorality, homosexuality, femininity, and lack of taxes, and recruiting of German's tribe people as soldiers in their army. Rome attempted to grant the German's tribes who had settled in Roman's territories the same rights as Roman's citizens, but they failed. The Roman's citizens were told that they were racially superior to the German tribe people and the Roman's citizens mistreated the their new neighbors.

The concept of American's Exceptionalism is not a new concept. Every civilization have believed that Their country was superior to their neighbors and they were racially superior to their neighbors. The British's Empire English's citizen was led to believe that they were racially superior to all of the people of color that their Empire conquered and were oppressing. The German Empire under Adolphe Hitler enslaved European people and begin a racist campaign to exterminate Jewish People in 1939 through 1945. The new American Republic also begin a racist campaign of extermination of all Native people (1862-1890, Buried My Heart At Wound Knee, 1970, Dee Brown).

In 1944 The German Army begin a military campaign to destroy the French Partisans under Klaus Barbie and Lieutenant entered the French City of Lyon executed thousands of French's villagers.

KLAUS BARBIE WAS A NAZI OFFICER IN T HE GERMAN'S GESTAPO AND HE AND HIS UNIT ROUNDED UP JEWISH CHILDREN, OLD MEN, WOMEN AND CHILDREN AND SENT THEM TO THE CONCENTRATIONS CAMPS IN POLAND AND RACIAL EXTERMINATION. KLAUS BARBIE SENT THE PEOPLE HE ROUNDED UP TO AUSCHWITZ A GERMAN'S CONCENTRATION CAMP IN POLAND FOR RACIAL EXTERMINATION. THE U.S. GOVERNMENT ALSO ROUNDED UP NATIVE AMERICAN PEOPLE FOR RACIAL EXTERMINATION IN U.S. CONCENTRATION CAMPS. THE U.S. INTELLIGENCE AGENCIES PLACED KLAUS BARBIE ON THEIR PAYROLL AFTER THE SECOND WAR (1939-1945). THE GERMAN OBTAINED THEIR CONCEPT OF THEIR CONCENTRATION CAMPS FROM STUDYING THE U.S. INDIAN'S CONCENTRATION CAMPS, RESERVATIONS SYSTEMS). DURING THE VIETNAM WAR A U.S. ARMY

UNIT WENT TO A VILLAGE IN VIETNAM CALLED MY LAI IN MARCH 12, 1968 AND THE U.S. UNIT UNDER THE COMMAND OF LIEUTENANT WILLIAM CALLEY AND HE ORDERED HIS TROOPS TO KILL OVER 500 HUNDRED VIETNAMESE VILLAGERS. CALLEY WAS PLACED ON TRIAL FOR KILLING THE VIETNAMESE VILLAGERS AND HE WAS PARDONED BY PRESIDENT NIXON IN 1974. DURING GEORGE W. BUSH INVASION OF IRAQ IN 2003-2009 ROBERT BALE A SERGEANT IN THE U.S. ARMY LEFT HIS BASE AND WENT INTO AN AFGHANISTAN VILLAGE AND KILLED OVER 16 AFGHAN WOMEN, CHILDREN, AND OLD MEN WHO WERE NON- COMBATANTS. IN MARCH, 2003 THE U.S. ARMY RAN A PRISON IN IRAQ IN WHICH THE U.S. TROOPS TORTURED, SEXUALLY, AND MURDERED IRAQ'S PRISONERS UNDER THEIR CONTROL. THE PRISON WAS CALLED ABU GHRAIB WHICH WAS A FORMER IRAQ'S PRISON. ON NOVEMBER 11,2005 A U.S. MARINE UNIT WENT INTO A VILLAGE IN IRAQ CALLED HADITHA AND THE U.S. MARINE MUR-DERED OVER 24 WOMEN, CHILDREN AND OLD MEN. ON DECEMBER 2,2006 8 MARINES WERE CHARGED WITH WAR CRIMES. ON JUNE 12, 202008 ALL OF THE CHARGES WERE DROPPED AGAINST THE MARINES. THE ONLY REMAINING MARINE CHARGED WAS SERGEANT FRANK WUTERICH. SERGEANT WUTERICH WAS CONVICTED OF A SINGLE CHARGE OF DERELICTION OF DUTY. SERGEANT WUTERICH RE-CEIVED A RANK REDUCTION, AND A PAY CUT, AND HE AVOIDED JAIL TIME. THE U.S. ARMY IN THEIR SENTENCING OF SERGEANT WUTE-RICH WAS STATING THAT THE LIVES OF PEOPLE OF COLOR WAS CLEARLY UNIMPORTANT. THE U.S. ARMY COULD KILL AFGHANISTAN PEOPLE AND NOT RECEIVE PUNISHMENT. KLAUS BARBIE WAS SEN-TENCED TO LIFE IN PRISON IN 1987 FOR MURDERING THE THOU-SAND OF FRENCH PEOPLE IN LYON, FRANCE IN 1944 AND SENDING THE REST TO AUSCHWIZ CONCENTRATION CAMP FOR EXTERMINA-TION IN 1944. KLAUS BARBIE THE BUTCHER OF LYON DIED IN PRISON DIED IN PRISON IN 1991 OF CANCER. THE U.S. ARMY NEVER PUNISHED THEIR SOLDIERS FOR KILLING AND MURDERING POOR VILLAGERS IN

VIETNAM, NOR THEIR KILLING OF POOR PEOPLE OF COLOR IN AF-
GHANISTAN AND IRAQ. ON JULY, 2019 A U.S,. SPECIAL FORCE SOLDIER
WAS CHARGED IN SAN DIEGO FOR MURDERING A TEENAGER ISIS
FIGHTER AND HE WAS FOUNDED NOT GUILTY OF KILLING THE TEEN-
AGER. THE ONLY PUNISHED HE RECEIVED WAS A REDUCTION IN RANK
AND PAY FOR TAKING A VIDEO WITH THE DIED TEENAGER 'S BODY.
IN THE U.S. THE CRIMINAL JUSTICE SYSTEM RARELY PUNISHED
WHITE POLICE OFFERS FOR KILLING AND MURDERING POOR BLACK
AND BROWN PEOPLE OF COLOR IN THE AMERICA. THE UNITED
STATES SINCE ITS FOUNDING HAS CARRIED ON A CAMPAIGN OF IN-
TERNAL AND EXTERNAL KILLING AND MURDERING THEIR CITIZENS
OF COLOR SINCE 1787. THE CAMPAIGN OF WHITE POLICE OFFERS
KILLING PEOPLE OF COLOR WILL CONTINUE TO THE END OF THE
U.S. EMPIRE. THE FOUNDING FATHER BEGIN THE CAMPAIGN OF LA-
BELING AND ENSLAVING AND OPPRESSING PEOPLE OF COLOR
WHICH HAS CONTINUED INTO THE 21TH FIRST CENTURY. THE U.S.
EMPIRE WILL END IN RACIAL CRISIS AND THE INTERNAL RACIST
PROBLEM WILL DESTROY THE U.S. EMPIRE.

PRESIDENT DONALD TRUMP RACIST HATE
TOWARD FOUR U.S. CONGRESSWOMEN OF COLOR

PRESIDENT DONALD TRUMP WAS ELECTED IN 2016 AS A RESULT OF
HIS CAMPAIGN OF RACIST HATRED OF PEOPLE OF COLOR AND PAR-
TICULARLY HIS RACIST HATRED TOWARD PRESIDENT OBAMA. ADOL-
PHE HITLER WAS ELECTED CHANCELLOR OF GERMANY IN 1939 BY
HIS RACIST HATRED TOWARD GERMAN'S JEWISH POPULATION. PRES-
IDENT TRUMP HAS A LONG HISTORY OF EXPLOITATION OF WOMEN
AND LABELING WOMEN AS INFERIOR TO HIM AND OTHER WHITE
RACIST WHITE AMERICAN'S PRIVILEGED WHITE MALES. ADOLPHE
HITLER USED THE RACE CARD TO WIN THE GERMAN'S CHANCEL-
LORSHIP IN 1939. PRESIDENT TRUMP ALSO UTILIZED HITLER'S PLAY

BOOK BY LABELING WOMEN AS INFERIOR AND JEWS AS THE OTHER AND THAT JEWS WERE THE SOURCE OF ALL OF THE PROBLEMS AND CRIME IN THE GERMANY.

IN 2018 THE MID TERM ELECTION IN AMERICA FOUR WOMEN OF COLOR WERE ELECTED. CONGRESS WOMAN ALEXANDRIA OCASIO CORTEX FROM NEW YORK, CONGRESSWOMAN RASHIDA TILAB WHO IS OF PALESTINIAN RACE AND CULTURE BACKGROUND FROM MICHIGAN, CONGRESSWOMAN ILHAN OMAR FROM MINNESOTA, AND CONGRESSWOMAN AYANNA PRESSLEY FROM MASSACHUSETTS. THESE FOUR BRACE WOMEN HAVE CHALLENGED PRESIDENT'S RACIST HATE CAMPAIGN AGAINST POOR PEOPLE FROM CENTRAL SOUTH AMERICAN SEEKING REFUGE AND OPPORTUNITIES TO IMPROVE THEIR LIVES (THE U.S. CIA AND THE U.S. PRESIDENTS EISENHOWER, RICHARD NIXON OVERTHROWING OF CENTRAL AND SOUTH AMERICAN'S GOVERNMENTS CAUSED THE IMMIGRANT PROBLEM AT THE U.S. BORDERS). PRESIDENT TRUMP CURRENTLY HAS HUNDREDS OF THOUSAND OF PEOPLE INCARCERATED IN CAGES AT THE TEXAS AND MEXICO BORDERS. AMERICA RACIST PRESIDENTS

AMERICAN'S PRESIDENTS HAVE A LONG HISTORY OF RACISM. GEORGE WASHINGTON THE FIRST AMERICAN PRESIDENT WAS A OWNER OF HUNDREDS OF BLACK PEOPLE AS SLAVES ON HIS PLANTATION IN VIRGINIA. DURING THE REVOLUTIONARY WAR 1776-1781 THE BRITISH HAD BEGIN RECRUITING BLACK PEOPLE AS SOLDIERS IN THE BRITISH'S ARMY. THE BRITISH PROMISED THE BLACK PEOPLE WHO WERE SLAVES THAT IF THEY JOINED THE BRITISH'S CAUSE AND FIGHT AGAINST THE REBELLIOUS AMERICAN COLONISTS THEN THE BRITISH WOULD GRANT THEM FREEDOM FROM SLAVERY. GEORGE WASHINGTON ASKED THE CONTINENTAL CONGRESS FOR THE PERMISSION TO RECRUIT BLACK MEN INTO THE AMERICAN' ARMY. WASHINGTON PROMISED THE BLACK MEN THAT HE WOULD GRANT THEM FREEDOM IF THEY JOINED THE CONTINENTAL AMERICAN'S ARMY. WHEN THE BRITISH SURRENDERED GEORGE WASHINGTON

DID NOT KEEP HIS COMMITMENT TO THE BLACK SOLDIERS TO GRANT THEM THEIR FREEDOM AS A RESULT THEIR SERVICING IN THE AMERICAN CONTINENTAL ARMY. GEORGE WASHINGTON DID NOT HONOR HIS COMMITMENT TO FREEING THE BLACK MEN WHO WERE SLAVES AND WHO HAD SERVED IN AMERICAN CONTINENTAL ARMY.. ALL OF THE WHITE FOUNDING FATHERS WERE SLAVE OWNERS INCLUDING GEORGE WASHINGTON. THOMAS JEFFERSON OWNED BLACK PEOPLE AS SLAVES. JEFFERSON WROTE SCHOLARLY PAPERS IN WHICH HE STATED THAT BLACK PEOPLE WERE INFERIOR TO WHITE PEOPLE. PRESIDENT JAMES MADISON WAS ALSO A SLAVE OWNER. JAMES MONROE WAS A OWNER OF BLACK PEOPLE AS SLAVES, PRESIDENT JAMES POLK WAS A WHITE SOUTHERN MALE WHO OWNED SLAVES AND HE CONSPIRED WITH SOUTHERN WHITE SLAVES HOLDERS TO START A WAR WITH MEXICO FOR THE PURPOSE OF EXPANDING SLAVERY INTO MEXICO'S TERRITORIES OF CALIFOR-NIA, TEXAS, UTAH, ARIZONA, AND COLORADO. BEFORE THE WAR WITH MEXICO IN 1846-1848 SOUTHERN SLAVER HOLDERS SLAVES WERE ESCAPING INTO MEXICO. MEXICO IN 1829 CONSTITUTION HAD MADE SLAVERY ILLEGAL. MEXICO WAS WELCOMING THE RUNAWAY SLAVES FROM THE AMERICAN SOUTHERN STATES. THE WHITE SLAVE HOLDERS WERE LOSING THEIR SLAVE S WHICH WERE VALUABLE PROPERTY. ANDREW JACKSON OWNED BLACK PEOPLE AS SLAVES. PRESIDENT JOHN ADAMS WAS THE ONLY AMERICAN PRESIDENT WHO DID NOT OWN BLACK PEOPLE AS SLAVES BEFORE THE AMERI-CAN'S CIVIL WAR (1861-1865).

PRESIDENT Y. GRANT THE 18TH PRESIDENT DID NOT OWN SLAVES AND ABRAHAM LINCOLN ALSO DID NOT OWN BLACK PEOPLE AS SLAVES. PRESIDENT GRANT INHERITED A BLACK PERSON AS A SLAVE FROM HIS WIFE FAMILY. PRESIDENT GRANT TOOK HIS SLAVE TO THE COUNTY SEAT AND GRANTED THE BLACK MAN HIS FREEDOM BY SIGNED THE PAPERS THAT RELEASED THE MAN FROM SERVITUDE.

PRESIDENT THEODORE ROOSEVELT WAS ALSO A RACIST HE BELIEVED IN THE PHILOSOPHY OF THE WHITE MAN'S BURDEN. GOD HAD ORDAINED THE WHITE MAN TO RULE THE WORLD. PEOPLE OF COLOR WAS NOT EQUAL TO THE RACIALLY SUPERIOR WHITE MAN'S CIVILIZATION. GOD HAD MADE THE WHITE MAN RACIALLY SUPERIOR TO ALL RACES OF COLOR. PRESIDENT WOODROW WILSON WHO WAS A PRESBYTERIAN MINISTER AND ADHERED TO THE PHILOSOPHY OF THE RACIAL SUPERIOR OF THE AMERICAN WHITE RACE. PRESIDENT WILSON PROMOTED AND SUPPORTED THE RACIAL SEGREGATION OF THE WASHINGTON D. C. (AFRICAN-AMERICAN WOMAN MS. ELIZABETH MINOR 1917-1996 WHO RESIDED IN WASHINGTON D.C. AFFIRMED PRESIDENT WILSON RACIST PREJUDICE AGAINST BLACK PEOPLE WHO RESIDED IN WASHINGTON D.C.). THERE WAS THE GREAT RACE RIOTS OF 1919 THROUGHOUT THE U.S. AFTER THE FIRST WORLD WAR WITH THE RETURN OF BLACK SOLDIERS FROM THE WAR IN 1918.

PRESIDENT RONALD REAGAN ALSO WAS VERY RACIST TOWARD BLACK PEOPLE. REAGAN DURING THE 1980 ELECTION FOR THE PRESIDENCY REAGAN RECEIVED ENDORSEMENT AND SUPPORT FROM THE KU KLUX KLAN FOR HIS POLICIES TOWARD BLACK AMERICANS. REAGAN BLAMED WHAT HE CALLED THE WELFARE QUEENS MEANING BLACK PEOPLE (MAJORITY OF THE PEOPLE ON WELFARE IN THE U.S. ARE WHITE PEOPLE). THERE IS THE RACIST STEREOTYPE THAT ALL OF THE PEOPLE ON WELFARE ARE BLACK AND BROWN PEOPLE.

GEORGE H. WALKER BUSH IN HIS SEEKING THE PRESIDENCY IN 1985 USED THE RACIST PROPAGANDA ABOUT A POOR BLACK MAN NAMED WILL HORTON WHO WAS A PAROLEE. WHILE MR. HORTON WAS ON PAROLE HE COMMITTED ANOTHER CRIME. PRESIDENT BILL CLINTON IN HIS 1994 RE-ELECTION CAMPAIGN HE SUPPORTED A CRIME BILL WHICH LED TO MASS INCARCERATION OF MEN OF COLOR (FURMAN V. GEORGE, 1972, U.S. SUPREME COURT PUT A HOLD ON EXECUTIONS IN U.S. ALL U.S. JURISDICTIONS WERE RACIALLY

EXECUTING BLACK AND BROWN MEN CARRYING OUT OF THE DEATH PENALTY WAS RACIST AGAINST BLACK AND BROWN MEN, FURMAN V. GEORGE, 408, U.S. 238, (1972), DEATH PENALTY IN U.S. WAS RACIST AGAINST MALES OF COLOR). PRESIDENT TRUMP HAS NOT BEEN THE ONLY CANDIDATE THAT RAN FOR THE PRESIDENCY THAT HAS NOT UTILIZED RACIST HATRED TO WIN THE PRESIDENCY. A MAJORITY OF THE MEN WHO HAVE RAN FOR THE OFFICE OF THE PRESIDENT USED THE RACIST DIVIDE TO WIN THE PRESIDENCY.

ADOLPHE HITLER USED THE RACIST DIVIDE IN GERMANY TO WIN THE CHANCELLORSHIP IN 1939. HITLER BLAMED THE GERMAN'S JEWS FOR LOSING THE FIRST WORLD WAR (1914-1918). WHEN HITLER WON THE CHANCELLORSHIP HE BEGIN A CAMPAIGN TO ROUND UP THE JEWS AND OTHER OPPONENTS WHO OPPOSED HIS GOVERNMENT. TRUMP BLAMED THE IMMIGRANTS FOR ALL OF THE CRIME IN AMERICA. ALL MASS KILLING IN THE U.S. IS PERPETRATED BY WHITE MALES (LAS VEGAS MASS KILLER IN 2017 WHO KILLED 58 PEOPLE WAS A WHITE MAN, IN THOUSAND OAKS, CALIFORNIA THE MASS KILLER WAS A YOUNG WHITE MAN, SANDY HOOK IN 2012 WAS A YOUNG WHITE MAN WHO KILLED 26 YOUNG CHILDREN, SANDY HOOK, CONNECTICUT). FOUR CONGRESSWOMEN OF COLOR TRUMP CLAIMED

CAUSED ALL PROBLEMS IN U. S.

THE YOUNG FRESHMEN U.S. CONGRESSWOMEN CONGRESSWOMAN MS. ALEXANDRIA OCASIO – CORTEZ FROM NEW YORK, CONGRESSWOMAN, MS. RASHIDA TLIAB FROM MICHIGAN, CONGRESSWOMAN, MS. AYANNA PRESSLEY FROM MASSACHUSETTS, CONGRESS WOMAN, MS. ILHAN OMAR FROM MINNESOTA ARE OUTSTANDING AMERICANS WHO ARE STRUGGLING FOR JUSTICE FOR ALL OF THE AMERICAN PEOPLE. PRESIDENT TRUMP WHO HAS TAKEN A PAGE FROM ADOLPHE HITLER'S PLAY BOOK TO WIN THE 2020 PRESIDENTIAL ELECTION. TRUMP'S ATTORNEY-GENERAL MR. BILL BARR HAS INSTITUTED

CAPITAL PUNISHMENT WITH IN THE FEDERAL CRIMINAL JUSTICE SYSTEM. MAJORITY OF THE PEOPLE ON DEATH ROW ARE MEN AND OF COLOR. THE U.S. HAS THE LARGEST PRISON POPULATION IN WORLD. THE STATES OF CHINA, RUSSIA, IRAQ, ISRAEL, CHINA, SAUD ARABIA PRISON'S POPULATIONS ARE SMALL THAN THE U.S.

CHANGE U.S. DEMOGRAPHIC

AMERICA WHITE MEN FEEL THREATENED BY THE NUMBER OF THE RAPID INCREASE OF BROWN PEOPLE AND PARTICULARLY BROWN MEN IN THE UNITED STATES. WHITE MEN ARE BECOMING MORE RACIST, VIOLENT, AND AGGRESSIVE. WHEN A COUNTRY BEGIN TO DECLINE THE COUNTRY BEGIN TO LOSE IN ALL VENUES

BIBLIOGRAPHY

1. Spence, Jonathan, D., (1990) The Search For Modern China, W.W. Norton & Company New York, London
2. Lawrence, James, (1994) The Rise And Fall of The British Empire, St. Martin Press New York
3. Xu, Guangqiu, (2003), Imperial China, World Eras, Volume 7,Imperial China, The Gale Group, Inc., 27500 Drake Rd. Farmington Hills, Mi48331
4. Hsu, Immanuel, G.Y. (1970-1975),The Rise of Modern China Oxford University Press, New York, Oxford
5. Kang, David, C. (2007) China Rising, Peace, Power, And order in East Asia, Columbia University Press, New York
6. Kissinger, Henry, (2011) On China, The Penguin Press, New York
7. Roots, John, McCook, (1978) Chou An Informal Biography of China's Legendary Chou En-Lai
8. Sir Foot, Hugh (1964) A Start In Freedom, Harper & Row, Publishers, New York and Evanston
9. Hearden, Patrick, J. (2006) The Tragedy Of Vietnam, Causes and Consequences, Purdue Press
10. Brendon, Piers, (2007), The Decline And Fall of the British Empire 1781-1997, Alfred A Knopf, New York, 2008
11. Tenney, Merrill, (1985), New Testament Survey, WM. B. Eerdmans Publishing Company Inter-Varsity Press
12. Bobrick, Benson, A Passion for Victory, Alfred A. Knofp A Division of Random House, Inc., New York
13. Roberts, Geoffrey, (2012), Stalin's General, The Life of Georgy Zhukov, Randon House, New York
14. Warren, Mervyn, A. (2001) King Came Preaching, Inter Varsity Press, Downers Grove, Illinois
15. Lewis, Bernard, (1995), The Middle East, A Brief History of the Last 2,000 years. Scribner, New York, London, Toronto, Sydney, and Singapore
16. Boatwright, Mary, (2004) The Romans From Village To Empire, New York, Oxford, Oxford University Press

17. Commager, Henry, Steel, Encyclopedia of American History, Sixth Edition, Harper & Row, Publishers, New York.

18. Bush, W. George, (2010), Decision Points, Crown Publishers, Crown Publishing Group, A Division of Random House, Inc.

19. Bobrick, Bensin (2012), A Passion For Victory, The story of the Olympics In Ancient and early modern times, Alfred A. Knopf Publishers.

20. Blackmon, Douglas, A. (2009), Slavery By Another Name, Anchor Publisher, Atlanta, Georgia.

21. Zinn, Howard, (1980), A People History of United States, Publisher Harper, Row Harper Collins, New York.

22. Corn, David, Isikoff, Michael, (2006), Hubris, Crown Publisher, New York.

23. Church, Winston, S., (1956), The Birth Of Britain, Dodd, Mead, & Company, New York.

24. Wright, David, Curtis, (2001), The History Of China, Greenwood Press, Westport, CT.

25. Dickerson, James, L., (2010), Inside America Concentration Camps, Lawrence Hill Books, Chicago, Illinois.